To Robert

STORIES FROM THE
WAR HOSPITAL

WRITTEN AND COMPILED BY

RICHARD WILCOCKS

June 2010

Published in Great Britain
by Meerkat Publications Ltd
for Headingley LitFest
18 Stanmore Road
Leeds LS4 2RU
headingleyhospital@gmail.com

Typeset in Minion Pro by DesignBomb
info@designbomb.co.uk

Printed and bound by
Duffield,
421 Kirkstall Road,
Leeds LS4 2HA

Attempts have been made to identify the authors of all the photographs in this book. Appropriate acknowledgements will be made in any subsequent edition should further information be received.

STORIES FROM THE
WAR HOSPITAL

CONTENTS

CONTENTS

INTRODUCTION

It probably took an hour or two to set up for the long souvenir picture in front of the main hospital buildings, and by the time everybody was ready for the photographer, the sun was shining straight into their eyes, on this fine summer's day in 1917. In the panorama all who worked there in any capacity can be seen, about five hundred of them, along with a couple of boy scouts and a group of out-of-focus patients watching in the far distance. 'Other ranks' of the Royal Army Medical Corps are standing on benches at the back, a swathe of nurses and members of the Voluntary Aid Detachment in front of them, all with spotlessly white aprons over their long dresses. Caped staff nurses and sisters are at the left and the right hand of the front ranks, where the officers are sitting on chairs. Nearly all heads are covered in some way, except for those of the Almeric Paget Military Massage Corps. Strangely, five women from the kitchen staff are sitting on the ground in the middle, right in front of the administrator, Lieutenant-Colonel Harry Littlewood, the Matron-in-Chief Euphemia Innes and the rest of the hospital high-ups.

I can identify them, and a few others. There's Mabel Whiffen, the matron, squinting downwards. Isn't that Major James Coupland, who came back from France in 1917 to take charge of the surgical work? I'm sure I recognize that one from a photo in Annie Storey's files at Special Collections in the Brotherton Library. And why is Sergeant Alexander Reilly sitting slightly apart, amongst the staff nurses? That face rings a bell. That nurse with her eyes closed, isn't she…

I admit it. Along with other researchers, I don't know anything about most of these people who gave their utmost to save lives a century ago, so a few will have to stand for many. It's the same with the men they treated. Records have been lost or destroyed, because of enemy action in the Second World War, because they were thrown away by people who thought they didn't matter or because of neglect. Young people often get rid of things belonging to their grandparents or great-grandparents because they do not value them, because they take up too much space or because they lack curiosity. It's a great shame, especially in the case of this hospital, because these people who gave their skills and compassion, or who suffered bravely both physically and psychologically, in a catastrophic war which shaped the modern world, should be well remembered. They should be examples to us in many ways, in spite of the differences between the society they lived in and the more diverse, less class-based society of today.

Without entering any debate on whether the First World War was 'necessary' or not, a few brief observations might be in order on things which have cropped up during eighteen months of research. I was startled more than once by the utter blankness about the conflict in the minds of many adults, but I suppose four years of new books, television documentaries and dramas for the Centenary should disperse some of that. I have discovered that historical research can be exciting, especially when something long-sought turns up like a golden key, and I have felt for myself that strange empathy with long-dead, apparently long-forgotten, people with which veteran historians must be familiar. I can now see, more starkly, a whole range of equivalents in a twenty-first century world full of xenophobia, warlords and fanatics, but also of peacekeepers and promoters of mutual understanding, and I have played the old "what if" game with added confidence. I have also noticed that the major contributions to the war effort of people from all over the Commonwealth, and not just the Anzacs, are being recognized much more than when I was at school, which is very healthy: black and ethnic minority children can perhaps see more relevance now. Their ancestors, too, knew about the defeats, the triumphs and the horrors. A million and a quarter Indians were involved, for example, of whom more than seventy thousand died.

You will not read anything here about what happened after the hospital closed. There was a smaller wartime hospital at Beckett Park again during the Second World War which was used as a training centre, military medicine has moved on in leaps and bounds, there have been remarkable developments in the area of prosthetics and treatment for what is now often called Post-traumatic Stress Disorder is rather different from that given to 'shell shock' victims. A fraction of all that would fill another book. A sequel, perhaps. The project started in July 2012, when four members of the Headingley LitFest team turned up at an event at the Leeds Museum Discovery Centre in Hunslet. Along with others with a strong interest in local history, we chatted to the organizers, from Legacies of War at the University of Leeds, found them to be not only efficient proselytizers but also kindred spirits, and moved on from there. We found a focus – Beckett Park, well-known in Headingley and beyond not just because it is now part of Leeds Metropolitan University (which has recently dropped the 'Metropolitan' and substituted 'Beckett') but because of its extensive grounds, where anybody can stroll or play. It is a significant part of the community. The grant from 'All Our Stories' at the Heritage Lottery Fund came through in the autumn, and research got underway. Very soon, visits were made to the archive kept in the James Graham Building at Beckett Park, to the Leeds Central Library, to the Liddle Collection in the Brotherton Library of the University of Leeds, to the National Archives at Kew and to the Imperial War Museums in London and Salford. Many hours were spent trawling through information on the internet, especially the records held on Ancestry. Valuable material was collected, to be stored on the laptop. Notebooks were filled.

But the most interesting information came from the descendants, the sons, daughters, grandchildren and more distant relatives who got in touch because of what they had read about the project in the press or on the website. Visiting them was a privilege and a pleasure. I was often amazed and moved by what I was told, and by the lovingly-preserved albums I was shown. They do not, for the most part, live in Headingley: one I could not visit lives in Australia, but I think they form a community in themselves. Hopefully, the stories which I have written up for this book will be interesting for not only local people, both transient and non-transient - many of Headingley's current residents are students - but for people everywhere, because they have universal relevance.

Thanks are due, of course, to the members of the LitFest organising team who have been constant in their help, encouragement and advice, to Sheila Chapman and Mary Francis, and especially to Sally Bavage, who accompanied me to the research room of the Imperial War Museum in London and who has made many valid criticisms and suggestions. Keith Rowntree, the archivist at Beckett Park, has been absolutely wonderful in answering questions, sharing in the enthusiasm for new discoveries and in providing images from the Sprittles Scrapbook. Similarly, the staff at Special Collections in the Brotherton Library have been impressively patient mentors during speculative visits to find something new. The Legacies of War team has been invaluable, because of the on-tap assistance it has provided, the courses it has run and the trips it has organized. It is difficult to pick out names, but Professor Alison Fell and Dr Kate Vigurs have been especially helpful, and Dr Jessica Meyer has not only given crucial advice but has contributed a major article on shell shock. She also delivered a session, 'Mud, Blood and Endless Poetry' for the 2014 LitFest! Alan Humphries at the Thackray Medical Museum was a walking encyclopedia, Oliver Bray was a reliable ally, and the three enthusiastic students from the MA course in Performing Arts at Leeds Metropolitan University – Katharina Arnold, Charlotte Blackburn and Hannah Robinson – who delivered a performance at the launch of this book based on three of its stories can only be described as inspirational.

Richard Wilcocks   March 2014

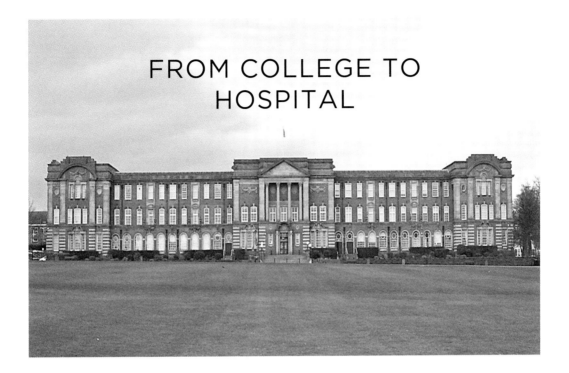

FROM COLLEGE TO HOSPITAL

Jack Pease MP had not got far into his speech before he was interrupted by a loud-voiced woman. It was the afternoon of Friday 13 June 1913, and militancy was at a peak. The front cover of *The Suffragette* for that day carried a front page devoted to Emily Wilding Davison, who had died under the hooves of the king's horse at the Epsom Derby a few days earlier. He managed to finish what he had to say after the heckler had been hauled out. President of the Board of Education, and a member of Prime Minister Herbert Asquith's Liberal cabinet, he had travelled up to Yorkshire for the opening ceremony of the brand-new City of Leeds Training College at Beckett Park, which had been finished the year before on what had once been called the Kirkstall Grange Estate when it had belonged to Ernest Beckett, Baron Grimthorpe, who had sold it to Leeds City Council to pay off his debts. The first cohort of trainee teachers (480 men and 300 women) had already been there for three terms. It was a pleasant afternoon, on the whole, beginning in the quadrangle with the grand march from Wagner's *Tannhäuser,* played by the band of the Leeds Rifles, unmarred by any serious incidents, though another suffragette was thrown into the new swimming pool at some stage and had to be rescued.

The buildings had been designed in an adaptation of a late seventeenth century style, which had been chosen by the energetic Leeds Secretary for Education, James Graham, who had also chosen the furniture and fittings, and named most of the hostels – Leighton, Macaulay, Caedmon, Brontë, Fairfax and Cavendish. Priestley was named by a sub-committee. Ironically, Pease in his speech said that the College was "a great possession for the city of Leeds" and that "it will be in the future a national asset." How right he was! Just over a year later, on the outbreak of war, the whole place was commandeered, renamed as the 2nd Northern General Hospital, and the Red Cross flag was hoisted. Suddenly, suffragette campaigning, union militancy and the fact that Ireland was on the brink of civil war faded as priorities, because the British Empire was at war.

In 1914, the summer was beautifully sunny by all accounts. Many wages were low, motor cars were rare, beer was a penny a glass, and cinemas, open all day, had been operating for just a year or two. Going on country walks, men in straw boaters carrying walking canes, women in ankle-length dresses, had become fashionable for those who could get outside the city, which was many-chimneyed and still gaspingly dirty, not very different from the Leeds which had appalled Charles Dickens with its smoke and filth decades previously, when he had visited on a lecture tour. Although there had been some attempts at slum clearance, well over half of working-class homes were back-to-backs, most of them of the older, insanitary sort with toilets in enclosed courts: the more modern sort, two-up, two down with a toilet block every four houses, were a minority. A rent strike which had begun in Harold Grove, Burley had taken place in the spring of the year. The city was well established as a centre for textiles, ready-made clothing and leather boots, and the local economy had diversified to include printing, engineering and chemicals. Beckett Park was a welcome green space some distance away from the masses of redbrick housing, and many of the houses around its edges today had not been built.

A conflict with an increasingly belligerent Germany had been anticipated as far back as 1907, when the Territorial and Reserve Forces Act aimed to provide a medical service for the Territorial Forces formed in 1908. Contingency plans had been made to set up a whole series of Northern General Hospitals, in Newcastle, Leeds, Sheffield, Lincoln and Leicester. Leeds was thought to be especially suitable because of its renowned Infirmary and medical school, and there was an original plan to base the hospital in the Leeds Institute on Cookridge Street, until RAMC Major James Faulkner Dobson took over command in 1912 and soon realised that this would be inadequate. He soon had detailed plans made to take over and equip the new college buildings in case of mobilisation, and on 4 August 1914, he swung into action. Beds appeared in the Great Hall and the library within a week, barbed wire fencing was put up in the Acre and flat roofs were designated as open-air wards. A week after that, six hundred beds were available with ninety-two nurses prepared to take duty. The declaration of war had come as a shock and a surprise to many, even after years of forebodings. Who would have thought that Gavrilo Princip with a group of suicide bombers (they carried cyanide) could have triggered off so much by killing an archduke and his wife in the faraway Balkans? The feelings of surprise did not last long at Beckett Park.

Very soon, all seven of the hostels were occupied. Major Dobson was the first administrator and Major Coupland the registrar. Lieutenant Colonels Barrs and Littlewood were in charge of the medical and surgical departments and Major Knaggs was in charge of sixty beds for officers. In April 1915 Dobson could not continue because of illness, so Coupland became administrator for a short while before leaving for France in June, when Littlewood took over the post, which he held until May 1919. Lieutenant Colonel Charles Edward Ligertwood then took his place. Major G W Watson was registrar from June 1915 to June 1919, and Euphemia Steele Innes, matron of Leeds General Infirmary, was matron-in-chief of Beckett Park and the war hospitals which were associated with it. Jessie Hills was the first matron, replaced by Mabel Whiffen, when she went to France in 1915.

Ninety wounded men arrived from the front on 17 September 1914, after the retreat from Mons. It was the first convoy to arrive at the now-demolished Midland Station and it was given a civic welcome. The Lord Mayor, Sir Edward Brotherton, met the ambulance train dressed in full regalia, and a dense crowd assembled in City Square to cheer the ambulances as they passed, on their way to Headingley. More cheering spectators lined Woodhouse Lane and the Otley Road. Some threw cigarettes and tobacco to the wounded men when they could. "They came with the soil of France upon their great-coats," wrote the hospital chaplain, Lieutenant Colonel J F Phillips for *Leeds in the Great War* (1923) "A few with support walked from the ambulance to the wards, the rest the stretcher-bearers carried. Some were entirely covered from view and of these some would not have been recognized by those who knew them best." A couple of months later, in November, more than a hundred wounded Belgian soldiers, sixteen of them officers, arrived. The sick and wounded were conveyed to Beckett Park and later to the auxiliary hospitals entirely by voluntary workers and voluntary funds. A fleet of two dozen ambulances was donated by various businessmen, the drivers men over military age, or in other ways unfit for military service.

Meanwhile, the College was obliged to rent alternative accommodation and to share facilities with schools, like Thoresby High School. The students who were left at Beckett Park were mainly women, because most of the men had enlisted. These were watched with great interest by convalescing soldiers, who no doubt made a few cheeky comments, in particular when they played tennis. Their behaviour – the women's that is - was described as "unseemly" by James Graham. Barbed wire separated students and soldiers, but of course this could be cut…

Soon, the increasing numbers of casualties made it necessary to open auxiliary hospitals. The biggest of these was the East Leeds War Hospital, which was set up on the site of the old workhouse in Beckett Street, now the Thackray Medical Museum next to St James's Hospital. Other auxiliaries were established in Bradford, Dewsbury, Halifax, Harrogate and Keighley. In 1915 it was clear that extensions and more recreation facilities would be needed at Beckett Park. A committee to raise funds was formed which included Littlewood and prominent citizens like Rupert Beckett, Joseph Watson and Frederick J Kitson. With some of the £26,000 which resulted from its efforts, a large YMCA recreation hall was erected, which became the venue for many entertainments, lectures and billiard tournaments. It was opened by Grand Duchess George of Russia, who was the Greek wife of the Grand Duke George Mihailovitch, a cousin of Tsar Nicholas II. She had arrived in England just before war broke out, and ran several hospitals for the wounded in Harrogate, like Heatherdene on the Wetherby Road. The funds also paid for seven hundred extra beds in a group of temporary wooden structures which formed an annexe to the permanent buildings. These extensions were opened on 30 March 1916 by Major General H M Lawson, and following the Battle of Jutland a couple of months later, the new wards were named after dreadnoughts and famous admirals.

Ever-increasing numbers of patients brought heavier responsibilities, and the whole range of operations had to be expanded. Pathologist Major Wilfrid Vining was put in charge of cerebrospinal fever (meningitis) and tetanus cases in the whole of the West Riding area. They were sent to Killingbeck. Typhoid, dysentery and malaria cases ended up with Captain Michael Stewart at East Leeds. In May 1916, a department for the treatment of injuries to the jaws and face was opened at Beckett Park with a hundred and fifty beds, which took cases from across Northern Command. Over two thousand patients eventually passed through this department, in which the consulting surgeon was Captain Maxwell Munby, assisted by dental surgeon Captain Alan Forty. They worked in cooperation with East Leeds, which had a department where dentures were made on a large scale.

King George V, accompanied by Princess Victoria, came on 27 September 1915, and again on 31 May 1918, when he presented several officers and men with medals. In between these visits, the hospital continued to develop: as the war progressed and the number of soldiers with healed wounds increased, it became apparent that large numbers of them were being left with residual disabilities. Injuries to nerves, stiff and distorted joints, bony defects and deformities called for orthopaedic treatment. In 1916, Beckett Park was chosen as a centre dealing with cases like this. A ward of about fifty beds was set aside, and a massage and physical exercise department was started, but it was inadequate, so in 1917 the whole hospital was converted into a Special Surgical Hospital specialising in orthopaedic work. 'Curative workshops' were associated with this, providing occupations which could be carried on and taught with the object of getting disabled men to learn in an interesting manner and to regain some of their lost usefulness. Nerve suture was performed on an unprecedented scale, along with innovative reconstruction work and bone grafting. New massage and electrical departments, X-Ray rooms and further extensions were needed, so another appeal for funds was made to the public, this time with the assistance of Sir Berkeley Moynihan. The £6,000 raised was soon spent, and the extensions were opened by the American Ambassador, Dr Walter Hines Page. Two American surgeons were appointed (see 'American Assistance') who were soon joined by others, so that by the end of the war more than two hundred American officers had passed through, many of them to take part in short courses.

The hospital had 3,200 beds when it was at its biggest and in 1918, 57,000 patients had been admitted with 226 reported deaths. I doubt whether this is absolutely accurate - and it can not be checked finally because of lost records. After the war, Beckett Park was taken over by the Ministry of Pensions, and the College was wondering when it could have its premises back. After negotiations, it was agreed that the hospital would retreat to the wooden extension huts and that doctors and nurses would be accommodated in Caedmon and Priestley hostels. By 1924, all students were back in residence at Beckett Park, but the hospital remained in the huts until 1927, when it was possible for everything to be moved to Chapel Allerton.

Extension wards 1918

STORIES FROM THE
WAR HOSPITAL

THANKS GEORGE!

Any local historian with an interest in the hospital must be grateful to George Sprittles, because of the scrapbook he put together. Images from it appear courtesy of Leeds Metropolitan University's archive.

Sergeant George Sprittles was born 1893 in Wakefield, son of a coachsmith. His family moved to Carlton Hill in Leeds, where he joined up in 1915. He was at Beckett Park until 1919, by which time he had reached the rank of sergeant. He kept a scrapbook of photographs taken by himself and by others, together with the odds and ends which tend to get categorized as 'ephemera'. It is the main trove of images for the hospital, and was once in the possession of his niece Joyce Pogson, Principal Lecturer in History at the City of Leeds and Carnegie College. She gave it to Iain Poole, who lectured at Leeds Metropolitan University, and he gave it in 2007 to the university's archive, where it is looked after by Keith Rowntree.

I visited another niece, eighty-nine year-old Margaret Sprittles, who lives in Hollin Lane, Headingley. She does not know much about Uncle George's time at Beckett Park, but she is able to talk about when he left. "After his discharge from the Army, he was ordained.

"He was a curate in Worksop until 1929, then Priest in Charge at St Alban's Church, Forest Town, in Nottinghamshire. In 1936 he became Vicar of St Michael's at Sutton in Ashfield. After that it was the Second World War and he was away from his parish as a chaplain with the Royal

Engineers in 1941 and 1942. In 1944 he was Rector of St Mary's on the Hill in Bulwell and Rural Dean as well. He was made an honorary chaplain in 1950: his black silk stole had a golden motif on it to show this. He eventually became Canon of Southwell Minster, and died in 1980.

"He was very popular, with a lovely personality, and he had the use of only one eye. He had a younger brother Harry who was killed when he was nineteen years old, and an older brother Joseph, who had wanted to join the Leeds Pals, but they refused to take him because he had had rheumatic fever, which meant he had a heart condition. He was told he shouldn't run for a tram! Joseph Sprittles became a well-known historian, writing lots of articles for the Thoresby Society"

In The *Blue Band* magazine, George is mentioned as a singer in a concert and as the MC at the RAMC annual ball in December, 1919.

George Sprittles as a chaplain in 1942

To browse through the scrapbook's pages, preferably by viewing them on screen in the digitized version because the original is fragile, is both fascinating and frustrating. Fascinating because many of the images probably exist nowhere else, and frustrating because many of them are unnamed, while the ones that do have names attached can often not be followed up, because of the absence of records. It was common at the time for postcards to be mass-produced from photos, and there are a few of these, for example one commemorating the visit of Lord French in 1916, which is divided into four little panels which show the interior of the YMCA hut, with rows of chairs and a couple of billiard tables, the scene of many concerts, Lord French inspecting men at attention outside the hospital and descending steps inside, with the matron, Miss Innes, behind him, and dozens of nurses crowded on to the same staircase in a photo which I have seen in other archives. Most of the photos are in various shades of yellow or brown, but a few which were given the correct amount of 'fix' during the developing process at the chemist are still black and white. Sprittles, is in a number of them.

He is seen near the entrance flap of one of a cluster of tents with other men in uniform. This is labeled '2nd NGH Camp August 1916'. Where was this taken? He is smiling with the Registrar's staff in several different photos, looking blank behind a table covered with a white cloth 'with Sister Pratt, VAD Habbershaw, A.Sheard, T.Shann etc 1916', grinning as part of a group of men sitting on and standing behind a garden bench with the mysterious label 'The Officials' and posing perched on a wall with an unnamed friend. Official visits to the hospital are recorded – Dr Page, the American Ambassador, King George and Queen Mary – and there are views of wards full of patients, some with cigarettes or pipes of tobacco in their mouths. Portrait photos of various friends, colleagues or acquaintances are in there, often signed 'Yours sincerely' as if they were sent instead of letters. There are comrades from the RAMC, patients in and out of hospital blue, nurses, VADs and an assortment of people out of uniform. Who were they? Who were Mrs Barker and Mrs Middleton, who paused by a tree stump in front of rhododendrons in 1917? Who was Miss Crowther, next to Sprittles at the main entrance? Who was the dapper man in a dark suit and trilby hat described as 'Woodie, assistant to Murgy'?

There are official group shots of officers, usefully accompanied by their printed names, and a portrait of the administrator, Lt-Col. Littlewood, also described as President of the Wounded Warriors Weekly Welcome, seems to be from a postcard. Dressing-up games were popular: Phyllis Russling (a VAD?) dressed up in a blue patient's uniform, with a cigarette in her fingers, and five members of the 'Cheero' troupe posed as four patients looking fixedly at a nurse, probably a reminder of one of their skits. The 'nurse' was Private J Hartley, an obvious wig under the white headgear. The others were Privates A Rostron, G Fryer and H Brown, and the photo (marked 30/3) was probably printed as a souvenir of the final performance in the YMCA hut, at Easter 1918, shortly before its members were posted overseas. Sprittles was fond of the popular Cheero Boys – lower ranks of the RAMC who became temporary entertainers, whitening their faces and wearing pierrot costumes. Rostron, Fryer and Brown are wearing uniform shirts and shorts (all holding cigarettes) in a portrait probably posted from Palestine, taken against what could be a shabby studio backcloth.

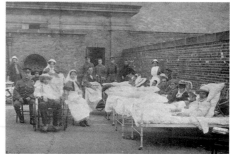

SISTERS MURGATROYD + PRATT "AWARDS 1916

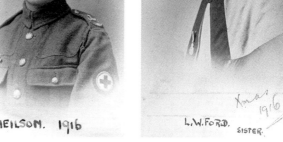

T.J. NEILSON. 1916

L.W. FORD. SISTER. Xmas 1916

STORIES FROM THE
WAR HOSPITAL

ROBERT BASS

I phoned Ken Bass after being sent his number from Features at the *Yorkshire Post*. He had read about the wartime hospital and wanted to talk about his father, Robert Henry Bass, and show me photographs. He told me he was ninety-one and that he could not meet me at his home in Scholes, on Leeds's western edge, for a day or two because he had arranged to play golf. "My father had nightmares, but he never told me anything," he said soon after I had sat down with him during my first visit, photos and medical records on a coffee table, my pencil and notebook ready. "My father told me, 'We once dammed a river and flooded the Germans out', but that's it, that's all."

Two particular photos drew my eyes – his father before and after a long series of operations. On 29 April, 1917, shrapnel had torn away his upper lip, some of his upper jaw and most of his teeth. "He'd been wounded before, the previous year, in the leg and shoulder," said Ken. "He'd been sent back to the front." Ken's wife Rita joined a conversation which lasted for an hour or two and, after making copies of as much as possible with my camera, I left to continue the research, promising to return.

Rita and Ken Bass   Photo: Richard Wilcocks 2013

Born in Suffolk in 1896, by the age of eighteen Robert Henry Bass was living in the village of Needham Market with his parents John and Mary, and working as a labourer at the New Explosives Company in nearby Stowmarket, which manufactured cordite. Just over a month after Prime Minister Asquith had announced that Great Britain had declared war on Germany because of the violation of Belgium's neutrality, Robert joined the Suffolk Regiment, on 7 September 1914, probably in the company of his friends. His record states that he was five feet six inches tall, weighed one hundred and seven pounds, and had five decayed teeth. Days later he was transferred, becoming Private Bass of the 8th Battalion of the East Surrey Regiment, which had moved to a base in Purfleet, on the River Thames in Essex. He received two anti-typhoid jabs there in December, and trained at Colchester and on Salisbury Plain. On 28 July 1915 the battalion crossed the Channel, disembarked at Boulogne and made its way by train towards the front.

In the trenches, it was relatively quiet for the rest of the year, with small numbers killed and wounded. Christmas Day was celebrated on 23 December, according to the battalion war diary, each man receiving two pounds of plum pudding. In the evening, about five hundred men were driven to the divisional cinema in the coal-mining town of Mericourt in lorries provided by the Army Service Corps and the Royal Flying Corps. Robert could well have talked with his mates about the widespread unofficial truces of the previous year, when opposing troops had mingled to trade tobacco, alcohol and souvenirs, and footballs had been kicked about in No Man's Land, but this year there would be no decorated trees, no exchanging bully beef for schnapps: higher authorities on both sides had issued strict instructions, and opponents were increasingly being perceived as less than human, especially since the use of poison gas. Commanding Officer Lt Col Powell wrote in the war diary for 24 December: "All thought of fraternizing on Christmas Eve was put an end to by trench mortars, sausages, rifle grenades and whizz-bangs on the part of the

Germans. Our artillery responded." 'Sausages' were observation balloons. Just before the New Year, new trenches were dug near the lips of a crater recently created by a large mine.

Nothing of any unusual significance happened in the first six months of 1916, with just sporadic losses. The main battles were raging at Verdun on the River Meuse, where the French were holding out in the ancient citadel town and where losses were immense. The scale of the German bombardments had been unprecedented, but back by the River Somme nothing as extreme was happening. There is no war diary available for the last ten days of June, but Robert was part of a long build-up to an offensive which, it was anticipated by generals filled with enormous optimism, would smash through the German lines after their barbed wire, redoubts and machine gun nests had been destroyed by the British and French versions of a bombardment on an unprecedented scale. The enemy would be tied down and unable to send reinforcements to Verdun. Robert would have seen at least something of the long ammunition trains, the camps for troops, the expanded equipment stores, the new roads, pipelines and telephone networks behind the lines. He would have heard the barrage, but could not have known how little real damage it was doing to wire which stayed mainly in place and to the enemy waiting it out in well-prepared dugouts and tunnels thirty feet underground.

Robert came out of the most appalling day in British military history wounded but alive, a day when, along a fourteen mile front from Montaubon to Serre, there were 57,000 casualties, forty percent of whom were killed. The 8th Surreys were briefed to attack Montaubon Ridge on 1 July, but before Zero Hour in the early hours of the morning, the assembly trenches were shelled, resulting in three killed and thirteen wounded, one of whom might have been Robert. When they did get to move towards the enemy, not all of them walked shoulder to shoulder into the sights of the German machine guns. Some of them were passing footballs to each other. The war diary reads: 'B Company started to move out to their wire. Captain Neville strolling quietly ahead of them, giving an occasional order to keep the dressing square on to the line of advance. This Company took four footballs out with them which they were seen to dribble forward into the smoke of our intense bombardment on the Hun front line.' This was later reported extensively in the press, with Captain Neville (who was shot in the head) depicted as a hero. Did Robert hear him shout something about "us versus the Bavarians" before he was hit by a bullet in the leg and shrapnel in the shoulder? There is no record of how he was taken from No Man's Land to an advanced dressing station, or even whether he was a stretcher case. Provisions for medical care had been carefully made, but for a tiny percentage of the actual numbers of casualties, and although doctors, nurses, surgeons and orderlies worked flat out, they were soon overwhelmed. Only three hospital trains were standing by, and an emergency shuttle service involving every wheeled vehicle of the back-up service from miles away was used to take the wounded away, which was nowhere near enough to prevent them filling tents and marquees, on and off beds and stretchers, in passageways and on the bare earth. When fresh ambulance trains eventually came to the rescue, the base hospitals became equally flooded. The most dangerously ill were kept in these, the rest put on to crowded hospital ships sailing from Boulogne, Rouen and Le Havre. There was often no time even to replace field dressings, and Robert may well have had nothing but the most basic treatment until he arrived on 7 July to be patched up by the RAMC at the 1st Eastern General Hospital in Cambridge, some of which was situated in Trinity College. He stayed there for just over a month. When he was discharged on 28 August, he was given ten days furlough, probably spent with his family in Needham Market.

On 22 October, he was transferred to the 3rd (Reserve) Battalion, and later to the 9th Battalion of the Essex Regiment. Robert was with them throughout the exceptionally cold winter of 1917, encountering wildernesses of frozen mud and filth, until he was wounded again on 29 April 1917 during the Arras Offensive. This was another attempt at a strategic breakthrough to end the stalemate. Hindenburg and Ludendorff had decided on a defensive strategy in the West, and had given the orders in February that German troops should be withdrawn in the Alberich Bewegung (Alberich Manoeuvre) to a new and supposedly impregnable series of fortifications and trenches which they called the Siegfriedstellung. As the Wagnerian references were lost on the other side, it was known as the Hindenburg Line. Robert was part of the assaults on this, which were often over ground where trenches no longer existed, having been obliterated by shellfire, where posts and dugouts resembled islands in a sea of sticky mud and where water-filled shell holes were everywhere. Some soldiers slipped in and drowned. Trench Foot was rife. The 9th Essex took part in the Battle of Arleux on 28 and 29 April, which involved British and Canadian troops. The battalion advanced towards enemy positions north of the village of Houlette, and it may have been here that the shell burst which caused the wound which would take Robert back to Blighty.

He could have blacked out after being knocked over, and may well have been brought back by one of those forgotten heroes, the stretcher bearers, who could have doled out a blue morphine pill and fixed a thin cotton wad under Robert's nose. Bearers were men of great strength and stamina – the stretchers, with sturdy wooden poles and heavy duty canvas, had an incredible weight even without anybody on them – but perhaps Robert was hauled on to a broad back, or simply led to the Aid Post, where the bearer may have filled in the Field Medical Card for the MO, who may have been busy or even dead.

Robert (third from left) with other patients from 'Jaw Ward'

Robert is recorded as arriving on 3 May at Etaples, just down the French coast from Calais, the scene of immense concentrations of troops and tented hospitals, well known as a place where final training in trench warfare was given, and where nurses and VADs were worked to breaking point. The next day, he was put on the hospital ship 'St Denis' (her name was 'Munich' before the War when she carried ordinary cargo), and his mother and father were sent a card telling them something of what had happened. He arrived at the 4th Northern General Hospital in Lincoln, where he was cleaned up and where he stayed for a month. Extracts from his medical case sheet are as follows: 'The upper lip has been severed… the front teeth of the upper jaw have been smashed… the tongue margin has been cut – he is able to open the jaw easily… bits of loose bone and tooth have been picked out… wound to be dressed with peroxide and saline'. A Major Shipman recommended his transfer to a special centre at Leeds for dental and plastic surgery, and he was admitted to the 2nd Northern General Hospital on 5 June,

after being driven up to Beckett Park from the Midland Station in Wellington Street by ambulance. He was now in the city where he would settle down for the rest of his life.

The notes on the case sheet continued: roots were found which could not remain, the full extent of the loss of bone in the upper jaw was documented and impact fractures were found in the lower jaw. For the next seven months Robert endured regular extractions and surgery, all of it under ether and chloroform. Intravenous anaesthetics were not generally available until twenty years later, and antibiotics were unheard of. There is no mention of any morphine. Massage was applied, a scar-stretching appliance was used, and part of his middle lower lip was rotated and united to the upper lip. Dentures were fitted in January 1918, but he was unable to use them. His parents, John and Mary, could have come up from Suffolk, but there were other visitors. Ada Porley was one of them.

Robert and Ada in 1968

Ada was sixteen when the War started, and in service. The idea of moving to Leeds became more and more interesting, because there was plenty of work there for young women. The city manufactured practically every weapon of war from cartridges and bombs to big guns, tanks and battle aeroplanes, and was the headquarters of the West Riding Munitions Area, which comprised nearly two thousand firms. But Ada was no shell-filler. She found employment in the clothing industry. Leeds was also the headquarters of the Northern Area Army Clothing Department. To give some idea of the scale of this, in May 1915, the Cattle Market buildings in Gelderd Road came into use as a store, and were filled end to end with 9,000,000 yards of cloth, and in the last year of the war the number of garments officially inspected averaged 750,000 a week. Helping to produce army uniforms was not her only work: she was also part of one of the many schemes to provide comfort and entertainment for the wounded. With friends, she regularly visited the hospital at Beckett Park, usually with flowers or sweets, and this is where she met Robert, who was nearing the end of his treatment. He decided to stay in Leeds. The marriage was on 2 October at St Martin's Church in Chapel Allerton, with Ada's mother Sarah and Robert's brother Maurice as witnesses.

Robert and Ada became the parents of three children. He died in 1969, aged 72.

Ken corrected me when I visited him again in Scholes, remarking on how well he looked for ninety-one. He pointed out that he was now ninety-two. We spoke mainly about the years after the war. "Seeing my sister Doreen christened in a church, that is my first memory. I was four. I don't remember my first day at school. I remember odd things, like walking past the Stead Leather Works in Sheepscar in the early morning, and the ginnel which went past Rakusen's . We lived on Christiana Street.

"In about 1926, I remember watching gun carriages being hauled up the Scott Hall Road from the barracks. The soldiers had riding breeches on.

"At Beckett Park they offered training for building, plumbing, painting and decorating and so on. My father chose painting and decorating and that is what he did after the hospital. The wounded soldiers did a lot of embroidery there, for chair backs and so on. They put nails in a board and wound wool round them.

"We always regret not asking our parents questions, later. In the Depression, there was often no work, like in the winter, but I never remember being hungry. I worked at Kershaw's in the Roundhay Road during the Second World War. We made gun sights and binoculars – a quarter of a million of them for the Army, and I often worked on nights to repair faulty ones. The cross hairs had to be made with spider webs, which we collected on a morning, because anything else couldn't stand up to the vibrations caused by the guns going off. The lines from the web were fixed with shellac. After so much equipment was lost at Dunkirk, we all worked overtime.

"You should write about my older brother Robert Joseph, who was born in 1919 and who went through a lot in the last war. He was at Tobruk, with the Chindits and in Norway when it was liberated.

"My father met Dr Vining when my sister Doreen was ill, first at home, then at the Leeds General Infirmary, when she was six. It could have been at the dispensary in North Street….well they recognized each other. He had been in the RAMC up at Beckett Park. My father said, "You did this for me".

"I can take that scar off for you if you want," the doctor said.

"No thanks, I'm used to it," said my father.

STORIES FROM THE
WAR HOSPITAL

THE STORY OF
DOROTHY WILKINSON

At his house in Edenthorpe, Doncaster, Dr Edward Huckett can put his hands quickly on just about any item in his extensive collection of old documents, memorabilia and antiques, which meant that he was able to give me access, within minutes of my arrival, to albums and scrapbooks from many decades ago. His mother, Dorothy Beatrice Emelie Wilkinson, was married twice at the time of the Great War, both times to an RAMC officer, and had been a VAD at Beckett Park. I was free to browse.

In 1889, Dorothy was born into a house full of music in Leeds, to her German mother Anna and her father Charles Wilkinson, a well-known local musician and teacher who had spent a year in Berlin and Cologne, where he had met his wife. Dorothy taught piano to private pupils in Roundhay, and often joined her father at prestigious concerts, usually at the piano. She kept the programmes for some of these, for example for a matinée at the Philosophical Hall in Leeds in July 1907 (vocalist Phyllis Lett, violinist Rawdon Briggs) which featured pieces by Tartini, Brahms, Richard Strauss and Sir Charles Villiers Stanford. She would have known Stanford well: he had replaced Sir Arthur Sullivan as principal conductor of the Leeds Musical Festival in 1901, and he had been the inspiration behind the 1906 visit by hundreds of members of the Leeds choral societies to perform with the London Symphony Orchestra at the Théâtre du Châtelet in Paris. Dorothy compiled a fascinating scribbled diary for this, during which most of the singers were seasick on the steamer to Calais and the train to Paris caught fire, with no casualties. In a scrapbook, in elegant handwriting, she copied the words of one of her favourite Lieder - *Mir träumte einst ein schöner Traum* (I once had a beautiful dream) - and put it near a Suffragette song sheet with her name and address across the top – *The March of the Women*. Next to this is a green, white and red ribbon with a badge attached, for the National Union of Women's Suffrage Societies.

"She was certainly committed to the cause," I was told by her son, "and she is known to have travelled to London for some big event, but we don't know the date. She told us that she had wanted to 'beat the big drum' on the parade." It is very possible that she attended the rally demanding votes for women in July, 1908, when one hundred thousand people joined a procession from Leeds Town Hall up to Woodhouse Moor, to be addressed by Adela Pankhurst (daughter of Emmeline), Pethick Lawrence, Mary Gawthorpe and Gladys Keevil – patronisingly described by the Leeds Mercury as 'a young lady with a winning smile and a most becoming hat' who 'admitted that some of the doings of the Suffragettes had not been quite lady-like, but she pleaded that they had done nothing unwomanly'. It is hard to imagine nineteen year-old Dorothy having much to do with the disturbances, over-dramatised as 'wild street scenes' by the local press, in October the same year, when Prime Minister Asquith visited the city, his meeting at the Coliseum in Cookridge Street protected against militant women by mounted police, with another open-air gathering of men going on at the same time in Victoria Square called by the Leeds Permanent Committee on Unemployment. The men and the women joined together, and there was a push towards the building where Asquith was speaking, but the only recorded damage was a smashed pane of glass, attributed to Leeds activist Leonora Cohen, who later became a local magistrate. In the same week, two of the Pankhursts were arrested in London for an 'assault' on the House of Commons. Increasing anger and frustration continued right up to 1914, when women's suffrage, unemployment and the worsening situation in Ireland became sidelined as national concerns, and when many suffragettes became enthusiastic supporters of the war effort.

Dorothy moved with her father to 'Greengate' in Boston Spa, a town fifteen miles north east of Leeds on the banks of the River Wharfe, at around about this time, and at some point met Dr Clifford Crawshaw Pickles for the first time. He came from a medical family: of his doctor father's six sons, five were also doctors. Clifford was the third one, educated at Leeds Grammar School and at the School of Medicine of the University of Leeds from 1909. He was a house-surgeon to Leeds General Infirmary, then resident medical officer at the Ida Convalescent Home in Horsforth. As medical inspector of school children for the North Riding Education Committee, he was stationed at Malton, where he had a commission in the 5th Territorial Battalion of the West Yorkshire Regiment – the Green Howards. In 1914 he was medical officer at Garforth Sanatorium, and served with his Regiment at home for a few months, but he was soon transferred to the RAMC, as a captain. He was needed urgently across the Channel.

Clifford Crawshaw Pickles

From late April 1915, Captain Pickles was the MO in charge of a casualty clearing station on the front, just behind the lines. He took with him a studio portrait of Dorothy with 'IF FOUND PLEASE RETURN TO CLIFFORD PICKLES CAPT RAMC 50th NORTHUMBRIAN DIVN 22nd FD AMB' written on its back. The 50th Northumbrian Division was part of the Territorial Force and had a headquarters at Richmond, Yorkshire. On 23 April, it was in the area of Steenvoorde, having arrived just as the Germans had attacked nearby Ypres, using poison gas for the first time. The Northumbrians were rushed into battle. The taps on tens of thousands of cylinders full of Chlorine had been turned on, and the prevailing wind was blowing yellow-green clouds of death toward them. No masks were available, and thousands – French, Canadian, British, Algerian, Irish – died horribly, the gas destroying the respiratory organs, leading to asphyxiation. Practically nothing could be done for the victims. In the months that followed, both sides developed increasingly sophisticated gas weapons, together with new forms of protection. By the middle of 1915, many casualty clearing stations, which were fed directly from aid posts and dressing stations near the gunfire, in this case by members of the 22nd Field Ambulance unit, had been supplied with purpose-built operating theatres and long, tented wards. Captain Pickles, wherever he was sent, would probably have assisted in some way with dozens of amputations. Decisions to sever limbs were almost always made at a CCS, and they were many, even though such operations were thought of as a thing of the past in civilian life. There are reports that surgical instruments wore out so quickly that cutler's shops were set up nearby on a permanent basis to sharpen them. Whatever the situation, it was too much for Captain Pickles. After three months, he joined the many thousands of men who suffered severe psychological trauma as a result of their war experiences, returning to Leeds suffering from what was then known as 'shell shock'. This term was first used by Dr Charles Myers for a paper he wrote in 1915 for The Lancet, though he did not invent it.

The medical authorities had little idea of how to treat this condition, which became widespread, with tens of thousands of men identified by the British Army as suffering from it by the end of 1918. In the early years, it was considered by some in authority (usually those who had not seen it up close) to be something to do with cowardice or malingering, or by a considerable number of doctors to be the result of shell explosions disrupting the soldier's cerebrospinal fluid. The war journalist Philip Gibb witnessed many cases at first hand and wrote about "… strong, sturdy men shaking with ague, mouthing like madmen, figures of dreadful terror, speechless and uncontrollable. It was a physical as well as a moral shock which had reduced them to this quivering state." Officers tended to receive better treatment. Captain Pickles was a severe case, according to his obituary in The Lancet in early 1917, but he was able to take advantage of a prescribed rest cure at Beckett Park, where he was visited by his fiancée. She would have talked to some of the dedicated young women there in nurses' uniforms, and admired them. There is no evidence of the full treatment schedule for the patient, but it could have included morphine.

In May 1916, having resigned his commission, he took charge of the practice, in the small Lancashire town of Earby, of his brother Dr Philip Pickles, who had just lost his life when HMS Russell had sunk in the Mediterranean after hitting a mine near Malta. Dorothy married him the following month, in the parish of Boston Spa. She was twenty-six. His health had been weakened permanently, though, and he died a few days before Christmas, at his father's house in Camp Road, Bramhope, near Leeds, of 'an attack of broncho-pneumonia following influenza'. It was normal for the principal mourners at the funerals of prominent figures to be named, and the list in the Yorkshire Post includes 'the following officials from the 2nd Northern General Hospital who acted as bearers: Major Jameson, Captain W M Munby, Captain A Gough, Captain W Gough, Lieut Sedgwick and Lieut Child.' A firing party from Pontefract Barracks was at Lawnswood Cemetery, and a wreath was laid on the grave from the 22nd West Riding Field Ambulance. He was thirty.

Dorothy applied to become a VAD – a member of the Voluntary Aid Detachment – at the beginning of 1917, and in March received a letter from London stamp-signed by Katherine Furse, the Commandant-in-Chief of the Joint Women's VAD Department, telling her at short notice that she was appointed for one month on probation to the 2nd Northern General Hospital and that she would be expected after that to sign on for six months. Her preparation was meticulous – she kept her pencil notes – because she wanted to be as self-sufficient as possible when she arrived. Her trunk contained not only regulation and non-regulation clothing, but also gumboots, a small oil stove, a candle lantern and 'one secure tent pole strap'. She would have read the list of instructions for VADs carefully. These included standing to attention when spoken to by an officer, Matron or Sister, performing all duties 'cheerfully and thoroughly' – these included sweeping, dusting, polishing of brasses, cleaning of tables, baths, sinks and utensils, washing of patients' crockery and sorting of linen in addition to nursing duties – and avoiding intimate relationships.

There is no diary of the time she spent at the hospital, but in her scrapbook there are selected entries from her autograph book, some of them from Christmas 1917. One of these reads: 'If you wish to rest near Paradise, just go and break a limb/ And be taken down to Beckett Park, where everything's nice and trim. /The patients there will greet you, and acclaim with one accord,/ Oh there's nowhere in the world so nice, as in St Vincent's Ward'. Another entry by a Sergeant Smith reads: 'May the darkest days of the future be better than the brightest days of the past'. The brief messages for 'Mrs Pickles' are all respectably affectionate, some wishing the Lord's blessings upon her. A Private Cook drew a pen and ink drawing of a young woman in an embrace, kissing a uniformed man. With the entries in the autograph book is a small card, published in Paris, depicting a Virgin and Child standing next to lilies, with the invocation 'Mater Amabilis - O Marie, ô notre Mere, faites nous part de votre joie pure et suave'. She kept the programme – in pencil, hard to read and on much-folded paper with a YMCA heading – of a concert by 'The Vincent Boys', none of them named, unfortunately. It is a rare find, because such things were normally binned.

Alfred Edward Huckett

At Beckett Park, as at most other wartime hospitals, there was a well-established belief that entertaining and generally amusing the patients was an important part of the treatment, which often gave civilians chances to do their bit, or RAMC members the opportunity to make use of a wardrobe of pierrot costumes. This particular concert, no doubt one of many, had about thirty numbers, and seems to have happened near Christmas, because carols were included. It was made up of sentimental and humorous songs, funny sketches and parodies, and beer drinking. Perhaps Dorothy played piano, and the programme has lines in it which could be from a script for a compere: "The audience are requested to leave quietly by the skylight. Stretchers and brickbats may be had from the Sisters… brandy for fainting cases is switched on to the taps at the ward end… vegetables may not be thrown at the artists, who are doing their worst…there will be an interval of sixteen years…" A quartet sang "Put me among the screens", there was a falsetto number entitled "Massage", one act was described as "an exhibition of high diving in the bathroom" and the show ended with a chorus entitled "Soldiers in the Dark".

The photos for this period are not all taken in wards: one shows what seems to be of a tug-o-war at an event in the hospital grounds, another is of a typically blurry group of men in uniform by the lake in Roundhay Park and another was taken at a picnic on a beach. One face recurs – that of a Captain Huckett.

Alfred Edward Huckett, one of the sons of a Congregational minister who had been a missionary in Madagascar, went out to France in June 1916 as medical officer to the 40th Divisional Royal Engineers, which were formed in Doncaster. He remained with them for twenty months, attaining the rank of captain. He was invalided out and sent to Beckett Park, where he met Dorothy and regained his health. He was then sent back to a base hospital in France, and was finally demobilized in early 1919. The wedding, which took place in July the same year at St Chad's Parish Church in Headingley, was a quiet one. There were three children, two of whom became schoolteachers, the other the Dr Edward Charles Huckett who has helped so much in tracing the history of his parents.

Dr Alfred Edward Huckett worked in Doncaster as a GP, and died in October 1948. Dorothy Wilkinson Pickles-Huckett died in 1974.

• CHRISTMAS CARDS •

Just about all of the regiments in the British Army produced Christmas postcards with patriotic and military-style designs and illustrations, which had become a tradition for them long before the Great War began. Cheerful Tommies are drawn helping to put union jacks on Christmas trees, smiling in trenches while they eat the puddings sent to them or beaming down dreamily from the sky on pretty girls back home as they wish them seasonal greetings. They were sent both to and from the Front, and were often saved as souvenirs of lost loved ones, which were kept in the scrapbooks of nurses and patients.

At that moment of realization I knew that I had been blind because I had wished not to see; it was only then that I realised, at last, that all these dead men, French and Germans, were brothers, and I was the brother of them all. (German playwright Ernst Toller)

STORIES FROM THE
WAR HOSPITAL

THE STORY OF
JOHN WILLIAM BATEMAN

"My father John William Bateman was on his back for most of the time he was in the hospital, in a marquee. He was a Second Lieutenant in the Manchesters when he was wounded." I was in Robin Bateman's front room in Chapel Allerton, just a mile or two from Beckett Park, where he had been the librarian from 1963-82, many years after his father's recovery. He had seen an article about the research in *North Leeds Life* magazine and had phoned the editor, who had contacted me. I was looking at pages of medical records and handwritten notes, compiled during his own research into his family, especially his father and his uncle – John's younger brother James, who had also been wounded. "After the war my father became a professional singer and I think he performed at the Leeds Grand Theatre with the D'Oyly Carte Opera Company, but why didn't I ask for details while he lived?"

Born in Kendal in Cumberland in December 1890, John William Bateman became a pupil at the grammar school there, but when his family moved to Armley, Leeds, he attended the new West Leeds Boys School, along with his brother, and became a lay preacher at Wesley Road Chapel. In 1909, he was a student at the City of Leeds Training College when it was still situated in Woodhouse Lane, and when he qualified as a teacher he joined first Ardsley Council School in Barnsley, then the Board School in Armley Road. He was complimented on his singing voice – a rich bass.

He joined the Army on 25 May 1915, training to become an officer with the Artists Rifles, a prestigious volunteer light infantry unit, and went on to the 2/5th Manchester Regiment as a second lieutenant. It was with them that he disembarked at Boulogne in February 1917, on his way to the front, to take part in the Second Battle of Arras. "I discovered he was in the 2/5th Manchesters, which was part of the 66th Division, after a trip down to the Imperial War Museum a couple of years ago in 2011," Robin Bateman told me. "The division was involved in the attack on Bullecourt on 11 April, and in the attack on Vimy Ridge between 10 and 14 April. He was wounded near there, at La Bassée, which is about fifteen miles north of Arras on the N41 from Béthune to Loos. I sketched a map of the area from the endpapers of an edition of *Goodbye To All that,* the autobiography of Robert Graves. He was writing about the La Bassée offensive of 1915."

Robin Bateman
Photo: Richard Wilcocks 2013

The Second Battle of Arras was a diversion intended to draw the enemy's strength away from a larger French offensive to the south at Aisne. It was successful at first, using new tactics and gaining a few miles after attacking heavily fortified positions, but by the end of the offensive much of the advantage had been lost, even though the Canadian Corps had captured the strategically significant 150 foot-high Vimy Ridge. British Empire troops suffered 158,000 casualties, the German Empire 130,000 before the situation on that part of the front reverted to stalemate. John was hit in the right hip by a bullet from a machine gun while helping a wounded brother officer, on the day when Sir Douglas Haig called a halt to British attacks while he waited for news of the French offensive.

John was taken back to the aid post, where field dressings would have been applied before transfer to a casualty clearing station. It would have been identified quickly as a 'Blighty wound'. John was soon receiving treatment at Beckett Park.

The proceedings of the medical board in late 1918 informs the reader that the bullet 'passed through the iliac bone and lodged in the sacro-iliac joint…' 'He has been operated upon on five different occasions and bullet removed together with some necrosed bone. In hospital eighteen months. General health fairly good. Movement of Rt hip joint good. Complains of pain in Rt buttock and foot of spine, particularly in damp weather. Is easily tired on walking… loss of muscle tissue over wound… inner scar (exit) 8 ½ ins long …' John was sent to the Kings Lancashire Military Convalescent Hospital in Blackpool, where he improved further after massage treatment. The official report states: 'The movements about the hip joint are good and the limb itself has regained its power to about 1/5 normal. Bending, jumping, or quickly twisting the limb causes much pain.'

Improvement must have been rapid after his discharge, because he was soon surviving well on stage as a professional singer. He married Lily Jasmine Bennet in December, 1918, and according to his son Robin, it was she who persuaded him to become a bass with D'Oyly Carte and later with the Carl Rosa Opera Company, and a soloist in many performances of oratorios. Due to the 1930s slump, he left singing and joined Odhams Press competition department in July 1933, contributing to its popular magazines *Titbits* and *John Bull*. He settled down with the family in Teddington.

Then came the Spanish Civil War. Perhaps it was his experience of the Great War which radicalized him, as it radicalised so many others in the postwar years. "Almost all his spare time after 1936 was spent on local Labour Party affairs, including street corner meetings about the Hitler threat. He also took part in work for tenants' associations which forced landlords to reduce the rents of some and do repairs on other properties, in accordance with laws which allowed maximum rent increases on pre-1914 properties. In 1941, he and Lily, especially Lily, worked with the Anglo-Soviet Society.

"In retirement, he took up painting seriously – his younger brother James was a Royal Academician, with his work in Tate Britain and many other galleries – and lived in the Lake District. I have a couple of his paintings in the hall today. I paint myself as well, and I sing, or at least I did until recently, with Cantabile, which is a chamber choir based near where I live."

Sadly Robin Bateman died 28 January 2014

The poet Robert Bridges was a physician at the Great Northern Hospital, in Holloway, London, until he retired in 1882, when he devoted his life to writing. He was made poet laureate in 1913, and his poems were set to music by Hubert Parry, Gustav Holst and Gerald Finzi. At the outbreak of war he wrote *Wake Up, England!* which he later wanted suppressed.

STORIES FROM THE
WAR HOSPITAL

FREDERICK CROPPER'S
MEMORIES

I had reason to know the City of Leeds and Carnegie College in Beckett Park in 1918 when, because of the 1914—18 War it had been taken over by the Army, as indeed were most institutions of this kind. It then became the 2nd Northern General Hospital, and housed the wounded. It became known as Beckett Park Hospital to most people and there are many still remaining in all parts of the country who remember it by that name.

The college was the property of the Leeds City Council and was the training college for teachers. It was residential, and the hostels were named after local and national famous characters. These names — Bronte, Macaulay, Leighton, Priestley etc — still exist, of course. I lived in Macaulay for some time, especially when I was an Orderly Room Corporal.

In addition to these main buildings the army had built a complex of asbestos and wood wards, incidentally all named after naval heroes or battles — Drake, Jellicoe, St Vincent, Nelson, Hood etc. There was a long corridor stretching between these ward buildings, extending perhaps for a quarter of a mile, and it was an interesting sight to see each morning the Commandant, Colonel Littlewood, starting his long walk up this corridor. With bent head he would say to everyone "Good morning", so that there was a continual "Good morning - Good morning - Good morning". He was the original of the Squire in W Riley's novel *Windyridge*. The actual Windyridge is, of course, Hawksworth near the moors above Guiseley.

The Ministry of Pensions took over in about 1920 and I was then placed in charge of the Admissions Office and remained there until 1924, when I left.

But the college had, some time before, returned and occupied the main buildings, so that for a time there was a combination of college and hospital. The hospital then moved to Chapel Allerton and the college resumed its normal life. During the Second World War, the main buildings and hostels became a rehabilitation Centre after Dunkirk, housing both Army and ATS. It eventually returned to its original purpose as a training college for teachers.

I came to Leeds to the Beckett Park Hospital in August 1918, having been marked by the Army Medical Board for home service after a period of two years in Macedonia where, like thousands more, I had malaria and had so many attacks there that so far as work was concerned I was of little use to them, indeed a liability as I had to be nursed myself. After a period at the RAMC Depot at Blackpool, where I was able to recuperate, I was considered sufficiently well to do hospital service at Leeds.

When I arrived with others at the hospital, it was to find a large busy place. I found that there was a canteen in the hospital where we had our meals, but that we had to sleep in St Chad's schoolroom on the Otley Road. Little do the children who attend that school now realise that there were rows of beds on each side. Later on I and a number of others were transferred to a house called 'Claremont' in Monkbridge Road. This had been empty for some time and was furnished only with beds; I do not remember any chairs.

The hours of work at the hospital were very long, 6 a.m. to 7.40 p.m. and sometimes later. It was an action of mine which later altered these hours. The patients in the hospital came from all parts of the country and had all kinds of ailments — for example loss of limbs, gastric troubles, shell shock.

There were indeed some really terrible cases. I was first attached to the limbless wards under Sister Stollard who was really a brilliant and capable nursing sister. She was also a writer and often made the leader page in the *Daily Mail*. The last time I saw an article of hers was in the *Dalesman* and I believe it was about Pontefract.

In addition to the limbless wards there were two wards devoted to medical cases. The limbless ward patients were there to get fitted with artificial limbs by the brothers Mayo who became famous in this field.

There were a number of lads who, despite their injuries, were among the most mischievous in the hospital, and some of them were frequently absent without leave.

Colonel Littlewood was very popular with patients and staff. There were many of the specialist staff of the Leeds General Infirmary at Beckett Park, amongst whom I remember Sir Berkeley Moynihan, afterwards to become Lord Moynihan. There was also Mr Flint, Dr Burrows and the brothers Drs Mayo, whom I have already mentioned. Dr Vining, if I remember, was a medical consultant, and of course there were many others whose names I have forgotten. Many hundreds owed their lives to the devotion of these men.

I cannot now say how many patients the hospital dealt with, but I think at least two thousand. This naturally made it a very busy place, especially on visiting days, and the route to the hospital was one of the busiest in the city. The visitors were augmented by lady friends of the patients, who always saw them into the hospital at night. These, of course, were the patients who could get out into town or, in the summer, into the Meanwood Woods or Beckett Park itself.

Another memory is of the visit of the then Prince of Wales, later Edward VIII, to the hospital. He was a grand lad in those days and very conscientious and thorough in all he did. At the hospital, as his visit drew near, all the extremely ill patients were moved to a separate ward at the end of the long corridor and the doors closed. But, unfortunately from the angle of the hospital authorities, this door did not escape the Prince's attention and he insisted on talking to every one of them.

Written by Frederick William Cropper in 1968, aged 76.

Sent to the project by his son and granddaughter, Eric and Jeni Cropper, of Bay Tree Cottage, Kirkby Malzeard, North Yorkshire.

• WARD NAMES •

The wards in the main building were known either by letters and numbers, or by the names of departments. The external wards, on what are now playing fields, were named mainly after famous admirals or dreadnoughts, for example Hood, Drake, Craddock, Jellicoe, Sturdee, Hawke, Frobisher, St Vincent and Beatty.

STORIES FROM THE
WAR HOSPITAL

THE STORY OF
LOUIE JOHNSON

Soon after war was declared, "men were walking about the streets of Hull carrying sticks over their shoulders and going to the parks to drill," Louie Johnson, aged eighty-six, tells the interviewer on a tape made in 1974. She is crystal clear as she recounts her experiences as a nursing sister in the Great War. In a calm, intelligent voice she remembers everything in great detail, how she trained at Hull Royal Infirmary for four years from 1910, how she was invited back to be a sister in a men's surgical ward when she had qualified and how she volunteered to serve with the Red Cross in 1915. The tape is kept at the Imperial War Museum, London, and can be listened to online. (Catalogue number 300)

She must have been very well thought of by the Hull matron, because it was an honour to become a sister in the place where you had just finished training, and the pay was good, at thirty-two pounds a year. Matron was against any 'home attachments', so Louie was discouraged from making friends with anyone, male or female, within a radius of thirty miles. A nurse's life had to be her work. Louie does not seem to have been too discouraged, though, because she got engaged to one of the doctors at Hull, a young New Zealander. When they both decided to play their part in the war effort, he could only sign up for a year because of where he came from, but she was in "for the duration" which would not be long, they both thought. "My mobilization papers arrived in a green envelope in May 1915."

She found the tetanus ward at Beckett Park "very alarming", and the work was completely different to what she was used to with all the war injuries, but her basic training was very relevant. "All their muscles stiffened, and they arched their backs… of course that was before the institution of the anti-tetanus serum… various doses were tried out on various men… and it was perfected.. a gunshot wound with not much to show for where the bullet went in is just as dangerous as a large wound… the bacilli live where it is deprived of oxygen."

She was soon sent to East Leeds War Hospital (main entrance pictured on previous page), an auxiliary hospital of Beckett Park. She describes its organization and layout as if she had planned it herself – yesterday. Situated in what is now the Thackray Medical Museum, the older part of St James's, it was large. She lived in one of several large rooms which were divided up into cubicles, with much use of curtaining. If a bath was taken "you had to sing". There were many ear, nose and throat cases and a large number of eye operations. The hospital had to expand as the war went on, taking over first the Killingbeck TB Sanatorium and then a couple of schools on the Roundhay Road.

She greatly admired the surgeons, naming some of them ("That Captain Gough –wonderful!) and describing what it was like to assist them, and spoke about how frightening it was when she was on duty as the night superintendent for the first time. She tried to sleep with the night nurses in a room above a working men's club, but it was difficult, because the children playing outside a nearby school and the sound of billiard cues striking balls on the tables in the room downstairs kept them awake. She breaks off: "I never heard anyone complain, because we saw so many things which were dreadful… and my fiancé at this time was on Gallipoli. My own brother was there as well, a mile away, but they didn't meet." She thought about who might be looking after them if they were wounded.

She gives an account of a typical routine for herself which must have been similar to that in other hospitals. The sisters began their day at eight o'clock, an hour later than the other nurses.

"I would go to the ward and get the night nurses' report and would go round the ward to speak to all the men and to see if anyone had died in the night. Then it was down to matron's office at nine o'clock to report anything different on the ward or changes in the staff." Back in the ward, she had charge of two staff nurses "and two St John's Ambulance girls, both volunteers" who took trolleys round and spent much time changing dressings, which had to last for a few hours at most.

There were three operating days a week, which meant that the night before the men had to be prepared, "with tincture of iodine and so forth, and no breakfast of course... I went down to the theatre with every patient. It was very frightening for a young boy to have a leg off. They asked me 'Will you be with me, sister?' and I told them 'I'm going with you and I'm going to stay with you, and I'm going to come back with you'... the surgeons were brilliant, and the CMPs used to come in to give the anaesthetic – that's for Civilian Medical Practitioners... there was not the same ease that patients have now with anaesthetics. It was ether and chloroform, unpleasant, with a lot of vomiting afterwards. Very disturbing for the patients. Anaesthetics were given in the corridor outside the improvised theatre. X-Ray equipment was "dangerous for girls" and this was known at the time: the St John's Ambulance girl who volunteered to work with it "intended to remain unmarried and to join a religious order."

"There were no antibiotics of course, so we had to rely on antiseptics," Louie continues. She goes on to say how they relied not just on strenuous efforts to keep absolutely clean, but also on "continuous drainage into tubes... and the use of antiseptic fluids...". She was describing the revolutionary new Carrel-Dakin wound treatment (see boxed item) which was responsible for saving the lives of many soldiers.

Convoys could arrive at any time, day or night, and everybody had to be on duty, ready. These, she says, were "terribly heavy days". Every man who could possibly be moved was sent to a convalescent home. These were all round Leeds, for example at Woodkirk and Cookridge, and were run by the Red Cross or St John's under a local doctor. Ambulances would be busy taking these patients away before the arrival of the new ones, and the staff would be attempting frantically to prepare an adequate number of new beds, but sometimes they could not: "I remember the Battle of the Somme very much indeed... There were so many they were laid on the floors and in the corridors... we made them as comfortable as we could."

They arrived wearing great coats or wrapped in blankets, a label fixed to a button at the Casualty Clearing Station giving name, number, regiment, nature of wound and whether they had been given the anti-tetanus serum, and if so, how many units. "It should have been five hundred units, as far as I remember. They had to have three injections at weekly intervals, the first one near the battlefield. It was copied into the book. There were no throwaway syringes like today – each one had to be sterilized, which took a long time...

They had a lot of lice, and there were three kinds at least. One man said to me, 'Sister, you mustn't come near me. I'm alive!' I told him it wasn't his fault. I never got any of the lice. There was scabies as well. You felt so sorry for them all. They should have been out playing cricket, or enjoying themselves with their families. That was the overwhelming feeling we all had."

She speaks about the dysentery brought from Gallipoli, and the many kinds of gunshot and shrapnel wounds, remarking that the one affecting the kidneys or the bladder were the most difficult. "One nineteen year-old boy had a dreadful wound, just near to the carotid artery in his neck. He had to be watched all the time because he had a bad haemorrhage. He never wanted to be on his own, even when he was getting better, and asked me to walk with him when he was out in the grounds. The wound altered his voice." The mortality rate from wounds was "not very high" according to Louie. More patients were lost to infections like gas gangrene. Bandages were hard to get hold of in any quantity, so wherever possible, the old ones would be boiled up, ironed and recycled.

Nurses were given the material for their uniforms, and had to pay for the making of them. A blue cape was worn indoors, a grey one outdoors, made of alpaca, a shiny, soft material. Louie wore a cap indoors and the prescribed hat when she went out. Two stripes on her arm denoted her rank as a sister. "I took off the cape for the operating theatre and put on a gown which covered everything."

Wartime weddings were not encouraged much, because of the expense: it was difficult to have a cake with icing on top because of sugar shortages, but she did get married. She tells of a few moments of panic when she lost her ring, which she used to take off and pin on her apron. All the patients in the ward helped look for it. "They were all saying 'Sister's lost her ring!' and then one of them found it underneath a bed."

She became an early member of what became the Royal College of Nursing, campaigning for the state registration of nurses, received the Royal Red Cross medal (second class) at Buckingham Palace ("Only matrons got the gold first class") and in 1919 visited her husband, who was stationed in Germany. The tapes finish with a brief account of her time there, in which she talks about helping a German family trying to cope with extreme food shortages.

Dr Alexis Carrel, a French surgeon, was working in a field hospital and laboratory close to the front line in the forest of Compiegne when he realized that there was an urgent need for a better way of sterilizing deep wounds. With English chemist Henry D. Dakin, he invented a system which would irrigate wounds with a sterilizing solution, saving limbs from being amputated. Carrel designed the apparatus to deliver it, and Dakin developed the solution. This had to be precise: if the percentages of combined ingredients was even slightly off one way, it would be either too irritating or would fail to sterilize the wound. It had to be mixed from scratch as well, and tested before it was used. The apparatus had to be mass-produced, and so did the pre-measured ingredients for the solution – in precise percentages, ready to combine quickly. In 1918, this was done by Johnson & Johnson, which produced the ingredients for the solution in two ampoules (sealed glass tubes and vials) labeled Package A and Package B, as well as ampoule holders, protective bags for the glass bottle, the rubber tubing, diffusers and charts needed to administer and track the progress of the treatment.

STORIES FROM THE
WAR HOSPITAL

THE STORY OF
JOHN PEARCY

John Pearcy came to meet me in Leeds in July 2013, bringing with him much of the material which he has collected over the years on his grandfather of the same name. Over coffee, he told me about what he has gathered, and showed me a substantial folder entitled 'Grandfather's War' which includes documents and photographs relating to troop movements, battles and hospitals, accompanied by his own commentary. This story is based mostly on his research.

John's home in Meanwood, Leeds

John Pearcy, born 1891 in Beverley, one of the four children of his railway plate-layer father (also called John) and his mother Annie, was brought up in railway cottages in Brough in the East Riding of Yorkshire. He became a 'domestic gardener'. Just before the start of the Great War, he moved to Leeds to work as a gardener for Mr T W Paul, owner of the tannery on Kirkstall Road, who lived in the rural suburb of Cookridge. After impressing one of the visitors, William Nicholson (later Sir), with the quality of his work, he was asked to come to the Yorkshire Dales to supervise the construction of a rock garden at his home – the fourteenth century Hellifield Peel Castle. This he did, on Sundays attending the local Methodist chapel, where a certain Jane Parker played the organ. She was the woman he was to marry – at the Methodist church in Settle on 20 February 1915. The couple came to live in Leeds at 9, Providence Square, Meanwood soon afterwards, John resuming his employment at Cookridge Towers. The following year, he received his call-up papers.

Their first child, John Robert, the father of the current John, was born three weeks before he enlisted in Leeds in 1916 to become a private, was posted to the 13th Battalion, West Yorkshire Regiment and trained at Rugeley Camp on Cannock Chase. Later in the same year, Jane Pearcy and baby John were back in Hellifield, renting the school house and looking after her ill mother. During John's period at the training camp, the 13th Battalion became the 8th Training Reserve and new service numbers were issued to the men of the battalion. With training complete he was sent to the immense Etaples Camp on the French coast, an ocean of army canvas, and posted to the 6th Battalion King's Own Yorkshire Light Infantry. He took part in the Battle of Arras and the Third Battle of Ypres in 1917. Transferred to the 3rd London Regiment in 1918, he fought in the Battle of Amiens, which was the beginning of 'The Hundred Days Offensive' during which the Allies, in an offensive planned by the Australian General Sir John Monash, eventually forced the Germans to retreat from the heavily-fortified Hindenburg Line and then from France. He was wounded by shell fragments to his chest during the attack on Malard Wood on 8 August 1918.

The battalion war diary for that date says that the attack began at twenty past four in the morning, and that owing to the thick fog, companies "somewhat lost direction". Four machine guns and over seventy prisoners were captured, but "a large number of HQ personnel... became casualties". Because of the disorganization caused by the fog and the casualties, "the battalion was unable to press on".

After a day at the 41st Casualty Clearing Station, John was taken to the tented First Australian General Hospital, which was situated on the racecourse at Rouen, then transferred to the 74th General Hospital at Trouville three days later, where some details were added to his medical records – "large abscess right thigh anteriorly below Poupart's ligament – abscess incised and drained". He was back in action with the 3rd London in October 1918 and was again wounded by shrapnel on the last night of that month while he was on operations near the village of Bléharies in Belgium. At the time he was hit, he was trying to establish a series of posts between the lines, and was spotted with the rest of the platoon while attempting to cross a canal. This time, it was much more serious. His life had changed for ever. He knew he had received a 'Blighty wound', and may have felt the emotions shared by many who had suffered in the same way, with a strange feeling of relief and happiness accompanying the pain and the shock, because now he knew was out of the fighting, for good.

Aid Post at Sailly-le-Sec in the Somme valley

The villages of Bléharies and nearby Rongy on the River Scheldt, a few kilometers from Tournai were devastated by bombardments during the German retreat, with many buildings turned into ruins and the main bridge blown up to impede the Allied advance. According to contemporary accounts, the inhabitants were evacuated in heavy rain, with roads ankle deep in mud, and household goods in carts and wagons, some pulled by emaciated horses that could hardly stand, because the Germans had taken the strong ones. British soldiers carried some of the burdens and handed out biscuits and bread.

John's right leg was amputated below the knee by the surgical team at the 3rd Australian Casualty Clearing Station, and on 5 November he was transferred to the 83rd General Hospital at Wimereux, near Boulogne, where he must have heard about the Armistice a week later. On 20 November, when he had recovered sufficiently to travel further, he was put on the hospital ship St David, a former Fishguard and Rosslare Railway Company vessel, and taken back to England. His next stop was St Anselm's, in Walmer, near Deal in Kent, a house which, together with Generals Meadow, another house next door, provided one hundred beds for wounded servicemen. Both belonged to Sir Charles Sargant, a former justice of the High Court, who agreed to the buildings being used as part of the welfare and nursing programme known as the Voluntary Aid Detachments scheme. The wife of Sir Charles, Lady Millie Sargant, became the hospital commandant, and the hospital was in operation from October 1914. During his time at Walmer he had a new amputation through the middle of his right thigh and an operation on his left foot, and stayed there until 31 March 1919 when the place was closed. He was transferred to the Royal Military Hospital, Shorncliffe Camp, for three months and then arrived in Leeds, nearer his Yorkshire home.

British Legion parade, Midland Terrace, Hellifield c1926

He was admitted to East Leeds Military Hospital on 11 June 1919 to be fitted with an artificial leg, but because his wound was still discharging, he was sent on to Beckett Park, where he spent several months recuperating. He could well have met Douglas Longmate, who was a specialist in the making of artificial legs, and he may have even taken part in one of the artificial limb races at Beckett Park because he was certainly amazingly sprightly after his discharge from the army on 10 February 1920. He had been home on special leave on several occasions and for Christmas in 1919. His grandson said, "Older residents of Hellifield told me they remember grandfather going around the village in some early form of self-propelled wheelchair operated by hand with a kind of bicycle pedal and chain arrangement.

Grandfather was one of the founding members of the Hellifield British Legion branch and paraded with other local veterans at the unveiling of the local war memorial in 1921, and led many Remembrance Day parades in the village. He must have mastered the use of his artificial limb quite well as it is said that while leading the parades he had to be asked to march slower as the band were having problems keeping up with him!" John became an active member of the Methodist chapel in Haw Grove, Hellifield, where Jane continued to play the organ, and in 1926 a second son, Norman George, was born. He worked on his allotment and she made a little extra money by selling home-made ice cream at local sports days.

During the Second World War, John and Jane, along with other members of the British Legion, raised large amounts of money to send parcels to local people serving in the armed forces. "One of those local lads was John Robert, his eldest son," I was told by grandson John.

"He was with the 78th Division in North Africa and Italy. On his safe return in 1946 he went to work at a farm where several German prisoners of war were also working. Grandfather and grandmother provided hot meals for these prisoners at their home, Bank House, and also provided them with warm clothing. This act of kindness was not forgotten, and many warm letters were received from the prisoners after they had returned to Germany." John Pearcy passed away in 1947.

John and Jane Pearcy at their allotment

• SMOKING •

Cigarettes are in many photographs of staff and patients, held in mouths or fingers. Advertisements in wartime newspapers for Waverley Cigarettes, considered to be better than ordinary Woodbines and about as good as Wills's Gold Flake, show a smiling soldier puffing away with the caption "What the man in khaki wants". They were 3D (three old pennies) for ten and one shilling and two pence for fifty.

The way I see it, when you put the uniform on, in effect you sign a contract. And you don't back out of a contract merely because you've changed your mind. You can still speak up for your principles, you can still argue against the ones you're being made to fight for, but in the end you do the job. (From *Regeneration* by Pat Barker)

STORIES FROM THE

WAR HOSPITAL

THE STORY OF

MARGARET NEWBOULD

Margaret Anna Newbould worked at Beckett Park as a nurse in the Territorial Force Nursing Service before being sent to the Mediterranean. She became the acting matron of the Formosa, one of the hospital ships which cruised up and down the Mediterranean, crammed with casualties from the fighting on the Gallipoli peninsula. Philip Newbould, who lives in Schlieren, Switzerland, posted me the results of some of his extensive family research (she was his second cousin once removed), which is included in this account.

She was born in January 1879, the third of the eight children of Henry and Elizabeth Newbould of Greenhow Hill, Yorkshire. By 1891 the family had moved to Thornthwaite with Padside, near Pateley Bridge, where Henry worked as a farmer and lime burner. Ten years later, the 1901 Census has Margaret working as a servant and cook to the Boyde family in Headingley. Samuel Boyde had made his fortune as a wallpaper merchant, and employed seven servants. At the time of the 1911 Census, she was visiting the parents of her friend Martha Morrison in Long Eaton, Derbyshire. Both women were documented as nurses.

Margaret Anna trained as a nurse at the Leeds General Infirmary, then became a qualified midwife hundreds of miles to the south: the *British Journal of Nursing* for 13 January 1912 states 'M. A. Newbould of Chatham Military Families Hospital successfully passed the Examination of the Central Midwives Board'. This suggests some kind of link with the Royal Navy, at the time the most powerful in the world. Soon after the declaration of war, however, she was back in Headingley, reporting for duty at the 2nd Northern General Hospital on 2 September 1914. She worked there for just over ten months, until she was sent to Egypt (24 July 1915) to join the Formosa, which was a Newcastle-built French liner, commissioned in June 1915 and adapted for the accommodation of four hundred and seventeen patients. It was one of twenty-seven hospital ships which were used for the Gallipoli Campaign.

This was catastrophic, and ended in defeat. Winston Churchill, the First Sea Lord of the Admiralty, had been the main enthusiast for the plan to attack the Gallipoli peninsula in Turkey as a way of breaking the deadlock on the Western Front. The intention was to open another front which would force Germany to pull some of its forces away from Europe and re-establish sea connections with Russian allies across the Black Sea. After hasty preparations by inadequately-briefed military staff, British, French, Australian and New Zealand troops landed on narrow beaches, many below almost vertical cliffs, under devastating fire from well-placed Turkish positions, thousands dying in the process. They fought hard to get off the beaches to move inland, but the war quickly reached a stalemate. Supplying the army was extremely difficult, and water was very scarce in hot, dry conditions. Enteric fever and dysentery spread rapidly.

Casualties had to be brought down steep paths on heavy stretchers or on muleback. As there were no harbours or proper landing places, the men had to be laid in shallow wooden box-like stretchers, two at a time. These were then loaded on to barges which were steered out towards waiting small ships. The 'boxes' with patients in them were swung aboard these by means of a crane (all under shell fire) and many of the small ships then made their way through the Dardanelles towards Mudros, on the Greek island of Lemnos in the Aegean Sea, where the larger hospital ships were waiting to take the wounded on to facilities in destinations like Malta, or Alexandria. Some casualties were treated in Mudros, for example in the tented 3rd Australian General Hospital: according to its Register of Deaths, most of the deaths there until the end of August 1915 were from gunshot wounds. After that, disease claimed the majority.

Few records remain of the medical staff or the patients on the hospital ships, but there are a few insights into their horrors. The Formosa was at one time close to the shore, off Suvla Bay. Margaret Anna is likely to have known Sister Ilma Lovell of the Australian Army Nursing Service, who is quoted by Jan Bassett in her book *Guns and Brooches: Australian Army nursing from the Boer war to the Gulf War* (Oxford University Press, 1992) as follows: "We were receiving wounded all night and terrible wounds they were—the majority of them were fly blown and septic. All were operated upon on admission and the little theatre was kept busy all night, —limbs, had they been able to have been treated before and would have been saved, had to be amputated."

H.M. Hospital Ship " FORMOSA "

She probably knew about the mysterious death by drowning of Lieutenant Peter Constantine Vassy, of the 9th Company, 1st Australian Division Supply Column, on 13 October 1915. He was drowned between Lemnos and Malta according to the record. Vassy, who had been a commercial traveler in Moonee Ponds, a suburb of Melbourne, before joining the army, was the subject of a Court of Enquiry, from which the following extract is taken:

Lieut. H.F. Wood-Hill, R.A.M.C. states:- I am Medical Officer in charge of sick and wounded offices on board Hospital Ship 'FORMOSA' lieut. P.C. Vassy, 9th Australian ASC, was admitted on board at Anzac on the evening of 10th October, 1915, as a walking case, and said to be suffering from influenza. He was berthed in Cabin No 13 in company with Lieut J. J. Moore, New Zealand Engineers Lieut Vassy had a rigor on night of arrival, temperature 105, but no delirium. The temperature gradually fell until the evening of October 12th and when taken about 8 p.m. it was about 100.2 and pulse 96. A careful examination by myself and two other medical officers (Lieuts Enraght and Sieveking) on the 12th instant, failed to detect any signs of pneumonia. In the morning of the 12th inst, the patient was cheerful and looking forward hopefully to his recovery and said he felt better. I saw him at 8 p.m. that evening and when first roused he seemed confused, but on talking to him he became quite clear and did not appear to be in any way despondent. I had no reason to consider the case one for constant supervision. This was the last time I saw the patient.' All evidence (from seven different witnesses), pointed to there being no reason to suspect suicide.

Lieutenant Vassy is commemorated on the Lone Pine War Memorial on the peninsula.

As from 1 January 1916, Margaret Anna (she always used both her first names) was given the temporary appointment of acting matron, and on the same day was awarded the Royal Red Cross second class for her work. The award, which was conferred only on women, was made to members of the military nursing service for 'having shown devotion and exceptional competency of nursing duties'. She was invested with this decoration by King George V on 23 May 1917 at Buckingham Palace.

She also worked at the No 19 General Hospital in one of the ports of arrival – Alexandria – and was Mentioned in Dispatches on 11 December 1915 and on 16 March 1916. On 1 June 1916 she was promoted to Assistant Matron, and came home to England to do temporary duty at the 1st Southern General Hospital in Selly Oak, Birmingham, before the matron at Beckett Park requested that she return to nurse there.

In July 1917, she was posted to France where she served three tours of duty until well after the Armistice. It is documented that was at No 59 General Hospital in St Omer, headquarters of the British Expeditionary Force and a main area of rest and recuperation, where she was working when she was Mentioned in Dispatches for a third time. From February 1918, she was at the No 73 General Hospital in Trouville and the No 6 General Hospital in Rouen before going to the No 42 Casualty Clearing Station at Douai. On 3 June 1918 she was decorated once more with the Royal Red Cross, this time first class.

A TFNS war diary entry written by the Matron-in-Chief, Dame Maud McCarthy, tells of her visit to the No 42 CCS on 12 May 1919 where she 'took lunch at the Sisters' Mess with Miss M Newbould, the Sister in Charge and her staff. Everything was comfortable, the luncheon table nicely laid, and the appointments good." She added that "the sisters were established in this very nice house which had been very much knocked about by the Germans". A month later, on 11 June 1919, the Dame reported that she arrived at No 42 CCS at 8.15pm and that, "although Sister in Charge Miss Newbould RRC, TFNS had received before 5pm information to the effect that we were coming, no arrangements had been made for our arrival. They were just finishing dinner. Slept the night

1.—Miss M. Newbould, daughter of Mr. Henry Newbould, of Pateley Bridge, and a local member of the Territorial Force Nursing Service, has been awarded the Royal Red Cross. At the outbreak of war, Miss Newbould was called up for service at the 2nd Northern Hospital, Leeds. Last July she, with five staff nurses from this hospital, received orders to proceed to Egypt. In August she was acting matron on a hospital ship, which position she still holds. We understand that it is for good work in connection with the conveyance of wounded from the Gallipoli Peninsula that Miss Newbould has received this great honour.

2.—Preparing for life belt drill on one of our hospital ships.

there." Next day, she wrote: "Got up at 9am and took photographs of the Sisters' Quarters which had been knocked about by the Germans. These quarters are in a good solid house with many good rooms not used. The house could be very much more comfortable if well managed, instead of that it was very dirty. There is lots of help here; the place is apparently not being supervised properly. The Home Sister was a kind little thing who provided us with lunch for the journey and nice fruit."

Margaret Anna was demobilized on 1 July 1919, beginning work in the Leeds Maternity Hospital in September the same year. For the next two years, she was in constant correspondence with the War Office and the TFNS about medals. There was some confusion over the RRC second class medal which had to be sent back on receiving the first class version, and she enquired about her entitlement to the 1914-15 Star because she had served in a theatre of war during 1915.

She was entitled to it, along with the M in D Oak Leaf, the British War Medal and the Victory Medal, which were given to all participants. She enquired about whether it was in order for her and the other sisters to wear medal ribbons on their civil nurse uniforms.

In February 1921, Margaret Anna resigned from the Territorial Force Nursing Service, of which she was a reserve, and wrote to Matron-in-Chief Macarthy for a reference, because she intended to visit her sister in California and might apply for nursing work there. Her sister Elizabeth and husband Frank Hodgson, a merchant, had moved to San Diego in the previous year. At the end of May 1922, at the age of forty-four, she sailed for the United States of America from Southampton on board the SS Homeric, arriving in New York on 7 June, then traveling overland to San Diego.

At some point she married William Arthur Morris from Kansas. In 1937, using the surname Morris and describing herself as a nurse on the passenger list, she returned to England on board the Queen Mary, giving a forwarding address in Edgware, London. The 1940 US Census states that William Arthur Morris worked as a restaurant cook and that Margaret Anna was housekeeper in a private residence, work she had done forty years previously in Headingley. Her husband died in San Diego in 1940, and she became a US citizen the following year. In 1942 she registered as a Democrat voter. She died in San Diego in January 1964, aged eighty-five.

> Probability is the enemy of fighter pilots in this war: there are simply too many things that might go wrong. The aircraft are easily combustible, the construction fragile, the engines weak, protection non-existent and the armament unreliable. They have no parachutes. The fact that engines must be hand cranked and do not have a starter motor means that there is nothing to be done if they cut out in the air. (From *The Beauty and the Sorrow* by Peter Englund)

STORIES FROM THE
WAR HOSPITAL

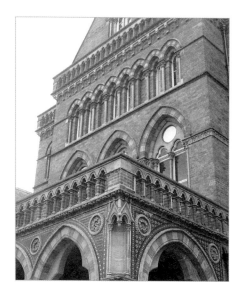

THE STORY OF
FRANCIS LEWIS

There is very little about Beckett Park in the Great War in the extensive archives of the Imperial War Museum, and not an enormous amount on Leeds, though the munitions workers at Barnbow and the production of cloth and uniforms for military purposes do get coverage. Browsing through online summaries of personal reminiscences which make mention of 'Leeds' and 'hospital', I came across one by Francis Charles Lewis, written in 1984. He had been wounded, and had an operation at the Leeds General Infirmary (pictured on previous page). There were possibilities there.

In the museum's research room, I found myself reading a fascinating, detailed, document entitled *Recollections of Active Service with the 2/5th Gloucestershire Regiment in France and Flanders 1915 – 18*. This took me from the moment he had joined up, with the permission of his employers, the Great Western Railway Company, after War Minister Lord Kitchener had called for half a million volunteers, all the way to his demobilization. He writes vividly about inspections, army diet, transit camps and life and death in the trenches, and he includes many illuminating anecdotes, for example one involving weighty gas cylinders being made ready for an attack on enemy lines, which had to be lugged into position while wearing gas masks at the alert position in case of a leak. The masks were of the early flannel type, and resembled balaclava helmets with eye pieces and a valve for breathing. The work was heavy, and the flannel was impregnated with a neutralizing chemical. When this came into contact with the flesh of hands or necks, the perspiration set up a reaction, causing most carriers to develop bad burns which rapidly became septic. Before these burns could be treated they had to be cleaned, which involved shaving the hair. "This was done by a brawny nurse with an open razor, not over-sharp. The poor wretches fairly danced with pain and before subsequent daily dressings were applied, some of them asked me to assist in removing the old dressings as the nurse could not spend the time to be gentle."

Francis, in a hospital somewhere in France after the first time he was wounded, was able to assist with this and attended to bed patients as well, "because the nursing staff were worked to the limits". He describes the VADs as having more patience and sympathy. After returning to the front line, he was wounded again, more seriously: "I thought I had been struck in the back of the neck with a rock… an orderly got me down into the dugout and stripped off my tunic and shirt and found a very small wound under the left shoulder blade, which he bandaged. I sat down and felt faint and had difficulty breathing and guessed something was wrong inside. I had the feeling that I would gradually sink away and die and lay down on the floor and became semi-conscious…

No stretchers were available and I was too far gone to walk. Four men started off with me, taking turns to carry me pick-a-back but I kept falling with exhaustion… we reached the first-aid post – another dugout 800 yards in the rear, crammed with wounded men. I was placed on a shelf two feet wide without sufficient room to lie flat, and had to sit with knees drawn up." After a long wait, Francis was taken by a relay team of stretcher bearers to a point where he could be loaded into a motor ambulance, which took him to a Casualty Clearing Station near Ypres, where two pints of blood were drained from his lung cavity. From there he was taken by hospital train to the tented wards of the South African General Hospital at Abbeville, situated on the slope of the hills overlooking the valley of the Somme. Here, he was prescribed a daily dose of port wine as part of the treatment, and given an X-Ray. Shrapnel was found in his left lung. He was taken to Boulogne for the ship to Dover, then put on an ambulance train bound for Leeds, where he arrived at the end of January 1918.

He was taken to a ward in a new part of the Leeds General Infirmary, as a patient of Sir Berkeley Moynihan. "He was a famous surgeon and had a special ward full of chest wounds. I was thoroughly examined and X-Rayed again and warned for an operation on 13 February but, after all the preparation, this was cancelled. Apparently, Sir Berkeley made Friday the day for these chest patients but, as he held a high position at the War Office, he could not always keep this date. I was again warned for an operation the following weekend and this time there was no delay."

Sir Berkeley told him that the operation had been successful, and that he had to clear the lung cavity of congealed blood, because bleeding had continued after treatment at the CCS. He had been doubtful about whether this could be done at first, but everything had turned out well, and the piece of shrapnel had been removed. Francis looked around him and considered himself lucky, because some of the other patients had wounds which had turned septic, which entailed a long spell in bed – either at the LGI or Beckett Park – attached to a Carrel-Dakin apparatus for intermittent instillation of an antiseptic though rubber tubes. While he was in the ward, Sir Berkeley removed a bullet from a man's heart, which caused quite a stir, because there had been very few heart operations at that date. Francis also came across a house surgeon called Flint, whose name was considered appropriate by the author after he had heard the probably apocryphal tale of a young miner who had died from heart failure and whose heart was preserved in a jar. The miner's widow was employed as a cleaner at the hospital, came across the jar and read the label, whereupon she fainted. Mr Flint was fetched. The woman said to him, "You have my husband's heart in a bottle", and received the reply, "I'll have yours too if you carry on like this". Mr Flint was well known at Beckett Park, for his surgical skills rather than his talent for repartee.

On 10 April, 1918, Francis was sent to one of the convalescent hospitals in the area, Gledhow Hall. This mansion on Gledhow Lane in beautiful grounds, painted by Turner a century earlier, had been offered for use by the authorities by its owner, James Kitson, later Baron Airedale, head of the Monkbridge Iron and Steel Company and prominent Liberal, at the start of the Great War. It was run almost entirely by members of the Voluntary Aid Detachment. Francis writes that he was well looked after there, and that the food was excellent. He found the people of Leeds to be "warm-hearted" and describes how the numerous large firms in the city took it in turns to entertain all the wounded in Leeds on Saturday afternoons, in the summer at the cricket ground in Headingley and in the winter at the Queens Hall. Beckett Park was the hub of a number of war hospitals and convalescent homes, and there could be anything up to two thousand to accommodate. Travel was free on the trams for the wounded up to 4.30pm, and every man who attended was given tea, a packet of cigarettes and the tram fare back to his hospital. Competitions and other entertainments were organized on a lavish scale. In addition to these regular affairs, invitations poured in from churches, other invitations and private individuals to such an extent that they almost became an embarrassment and (according to

Gledhow Hall VAD Hospital

Francis Lewis) it was frequently necessary for the sister-in-charge of a ward to detail men to accept these invitations to avoid disappointing some well-meaning, generous person. Every afternoon, the cinemas were free, and the Headingley Picture House in Cottage Road was particularly popular with men from Beckett Park.

After an appearance in front of a medical board at East Leeds Hospital, Francis was diagnosed as being in too poor a condition to be discharged, and was ordered a month's further convalescence at Saltburn-by-the-Sea, where he arrived on 25 May. A local committee had formed there for the sole purpose of entertaining recovering soldiers, and the programme included concerts and trips to the nearby Yorkshire Moors in horse-drawn brakes which normally included a good meal at some isolated hotel or farmhouse, where many of the items which were strictly rationed could be found. Francis tells the tale of a man with heart trouble who drank too much and became very ill: back at the convalescent home, the matron and staff became quite worried, because to serve a wounded soldier with intoxicants was a serious offence. Fortunately, the man recovered. A doctor examined Francis and his remarks were "Pale, poor but improving" at first, but on 26 June he found himself back in Leeds after the doctor had written "General condition good". A meeting of a medical board at East Leeds Hospital took place on 2 July, and his papers were endorsed 'Invalided', which led to his assuming that he would soon be discharged, so he bought a new pair of boots and ordered a suit of clothes.

It was not to be. On 12 July he was sent to yet another convalescent hospital in Cookridge, where he awaited the completion of the discharge arrangements. On 26 July, he was informed that any man who was fit for anything was to be retained to release fit men for active service, and that as he had been a clerk, it was the intention to keep him on in that capacity. He was bitterly disappointed: if he had not spent a month in Saltburn, he could have been sent home before the new order was made. After a spell as an errand boy to a doctor, he was sent along with other men unfit for active service on what was termed 'agricultural furlough', which involved flax pulling at Hambleton, near Selby. When the crop had been harvested, he was sent to Llanrwst in Wales, where he joined a company engaged in building new banks along the River Conway to prevent flooding. From there, he was sent to Ripon, which was a transfer camp which "…collected all the halt and maimed, men with low standards of fitness through wounds or illness." Here he was sent into a room in which several officers representing various corps sat at tables and men were brought in, graded and accepted by one or other of them. Francis had been warned by men who had been through the machinery that the officer who had first choice represented the Royal Defence Corps, which, it was rumoured, was being formed into units to be sent to Archangel to help the White Russians fight the Red Russians, an enterprise which was doomed to failure: the force was later extracted with difficulty after suffering severe hardship in Arctic conditions. Fortunately, Francis was marked as BIII, a very low category, by the doctor. Francis worked as a ledger clerk from then on while the bureaucratic wheels turned. He notes that "much valuable material was being disposed of dishonestly" and remembers an incident on Armistice Night, when free beer had been issued in fire buckets, with each man dipping in a mug: "A number of us were sitting round the stove and suddenly noticed a mouse swimming round and round in the bucket. One of the men, who happened to be a shell-shock case, grabbed the mouse, opened the stove door and dropped it in the fire and immediately passed into a deep faint." Francis was finally discharged from the army soon after he returned from Christmas leave, arriving home in Gloucester in the early hours of 22 January 1919.

STORIES FROM THE

WAR HOSPITAL

A

ROMANCE

One of the first people to get in touch with the wartime hospital project was Sarah Saunders-Davies, who is the grand-daughter of a nurse who worked at Beckett Park and who met her future husband there. She had sent an assortment of papers and photographs to Peter Liddle, to be placed in Special Collections at the Brotherton Library of the University of Leeds. Violet Trafford-Towers was the nurse's name (just Towers for most of the time) and Leonard Frank Rooke was the Lieutenant in the Royal Flying Corps, the air arm of the Army, who arrived at Beckett Park after a serious crash. Although they first met at the hospital, there is nothing substantial in the library records on how or where they met, but it can be guessed that this was beyond matron's prying eyes, because liaisons between nurses and patients were officially not allowed.

Educated in England, Switzerland and France, Leonard Rooke had some notable military ancestors, like Admiral Sir George Rooke, who had commanded the forces that captured Gibraltar for the British in 1704. An enthusiastic and skillful rider, he enlisted in King Edward's Horse in 1912 at the age of twenty-four, soon after finishing at Brasenose College, Oxford. This cavalry regiment became part of the Special Reserve, and was part of the general mobilisation in 1914. His father Louis wrote to him, "I wish you all success, and that the 'Flag of England' will still continue to rule the world. If we never meet again remember the last and fondest wish of your loving father is 'God bless you', and in due course – may you return to England crowned with victory". After a spell in Egypt, he was appointed to a commission in the Kings Own Scottish Borderers as a second lieutenant in January, 1915, going with the regiment to France and the front five months later in June. He was promoted to Lieutenant soon afterwards, in August. In his Liddle files are two testimonials to him from senior officers: the first of these, dated August 1917, when he was in hospital at Beckett Park, mentions that he led more than one bombing raid on enemy trenches, that he was 'a first class horseman', that he had 'great tact' and that he was 'very popular with brother officers and all ranks'. It also states that he wanted to transfer to 'Indian Army (Cavalry)'. The second is dated February 1932 and is signed by a Brigadier-General Elves-Coke, who describes Leonard as "...most conscientious, industrious and intelligent, well above the average in enterprise and pluck. He has a very agreeable manner, and I am sure he would be a success in a position of responsibility." A report on a grenade attack against an enemy listening post, which took place in November 1915, recounts how Lieutenant Rooke with six grenadiers were successful in knocking it out by throwing Mills bombs.

At Arras, on 4 April 1916, he received what was routinely described as a gunshot wound in the left forearm and was taken to No.42 Casualty Clearing Station, a canvas establishment which had been established at Aubigny-en-Artois in the Pas de Calais during the previous month. A piece of metal was removed from the wound which had, in fact, been made by fragments of a hand grenade. They left a gash three inches long and caused a fracture of the ulna. After four days he was transferred to No.6 Red Cross Hospital at Etaples and then to Blighty. He was treated at Queen Alexandra's Military Hospital, Millbank, where he received massage treatment, and was mentioned in Despatches for his actions in the battle. He healed fast, and was able to stop wearing a sling in June. Soon after this, he was seconded to 41 Squadron of the rapidly developing Royal Flying Corps. In spite of improvements, the aircraft used by the RFC were not particularly reliable by modern standards: to give an indication of this, in October 1916, eighteen aircraft from 41 squadron (Royal Aircraft Factory FE8s) departed from their base at Gosport for a 225-mile flight to St Omer, but only twelve of them actually got there, the others landing because of technical problems. The twelve pilots spent a week in St Omer before moving on to Abeele, where their ground crews reached them by road, and the remaining six pilots, minus their aircraft, arrived on a train. Leonard was under instruction in England at the time, and it was during this period that he came close to death.

On 11 December, 1916, at an aerodrome which used to be on what is now Doncaster racecourse, he climbed into a Maurice Farham Shorthorn biplane, a French reconnaissance and light bomber aircraft which had been introduced into service in May 1914 and which was already more or less obsolete. Similar planes had been involved in the first bombing raid of the War, on German positions near Ostend, in December 1914. He was a passenger, with his instructor, the pilot. As the machine was getting off the ground, the revolutions of the engine dropped. Instead of throttling down and landing back at the aerodrome, the pilot decided to keep the engine going, and tried to rise over some low trees, without success. He took the top off one of these before crashing, completely wrecking the aircraft. Both men were severely injured. Leonard was taken to Doncaster Royal Infirmary, where he received his initial treatment for compound fractures of the tibia and the fibula in both legs and damage to his nose. The surgeon there reported that he had lost a lot of blood, and wrote that " one tibia was broken in at least two separate places. Both tibiae and fibulae were fractured, and the damage to one was so severe that primary amputation was only just avoided

In March, 1917, he arrived at Beckett Park. There it was found (according to a Medical Officer's report written in October 1919) that "…there was much contusion of the limbs and at an early stage gangrene of one of them was feared. In the 2nd Northern General Hospital he lay for many months – one leg did well – the other did not become united and it became necessary to plate the tibia. Union resulted but the plate caused trouble and had to be removed. Though he has made a very good recovery, there can be no question of the grave nature of the injuries and that compared with what he was before his accident a considerable amount of disablement is likely to have resulted and some risk of occasional recurrent troubles probably still exists."

He seems to have spent some time in St Vincent ward, named after one of the dreadnoughts which fought at the Battle of Jutland, which was in a large hut in the grounds. The woman he was going to marry certainly worked there: in her postcard album is one from a sergeant working at an isolation camp at Catterick (who complains about 'the rotten weather') which is addressed to 'Sister Towers, St Vincent's Ward'. This means that Violet is likely to have known Dorothy Wilkinson, the VAD nurse who worked in the same ward, whose story has been told separately. Amongst Leonard Rooke's papers are two souvenirs, his portable heliograph (for signalling) in a leather case and the crest from a German soldier's Pickelhaube.

Souvenir crest from a German Pickelhaube

Violet Towers was a qualified staff nurse, a member of Queen Alexandra's Imperial Military Nursing Service, who lived in Priestley Hall at Beckett Park. Born and brought up on the Isle of Man, she came up to the Derbyshire Royal Infirmary to train for three years, beginning before the War started. When she left Derby, she had worked in the medical, surgical and eye wards, and had experience in the children's ward and the massage department. She brought her text books with her to Headingley, including her copy of Groves and Brickdale's *Text-book for Nurses,* which was later to accompany her to Basrah in Iraq in the early Twenties. Her postcard album includes a number of ward photographs, a commemoration of a visit from Lord French, groups of unnamed soldiers and patients and one or two of what could be rather spartan operating rooms. One of them is of buildings outside Gledhow Hall VAD hospital.

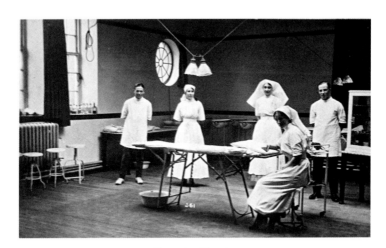

Operating Theatre

A postcard sent to her in St Vincent ward from 'Ginger' tells her that he is having a 'ripping time' and hopes she is 'having a decent time of it among the Drakes' – presumably a reference to nearby Drake ward. One from a Martin shows a hotel in Le Havre (Le Palais des Royales) with the message "Dear Sister – won't be coming home but am being sent to a 'home for lost dogs' 20 miles from here – so lonesome – miss you all." Another from a J W Budges, sent from the Thackeray Hotel in Great Russell Street, London, in April 1917, reads, "Having a giddy time already – dinner with Major Knaggs tonight!! Was enquiring very sweetly about Sister Robertson and staff. Two of the Canadian officers looked us up this afternoon. We are having lunch with them at the Royal Automobile Club tomorrow. Love to all in Vincent. How is the gardening coming on?" Major Robert Lawford Knaggs was responsible for sixty officers' beds at the hospital. Gardening was important for many of the staff and patients: there were competitions, and plots of flowers and vegetables near the huts. The Royal Automobile Club, not to be confused with the RAC, an automotive services company which it once owned, was (and still is) a private club. It ran the largest club house in London, built in French Renaissance style, on Pall Mall. Women were excluded from membership. The RAC contributed to the war effort through a force of volunteers which accompanied the British Expeditionary Force to France in 1914. Wearing khaki uniforms with no badges except for an RAC brassard on an armband (which put them at risk of being shot as spies if they were captured), they drove officers of the General Staff and cavalry division as required. Large numbers of photographs taken at Beckett Park, often with popular cameras like the Brownie made by Eastman Kodak, were turned into postcards, and there is one of these in the album. It shows Leonard Rooke in a hospital bed. The message is "Cheerio you old thing. Thought you would like this." It is signed 'Lal', which was Leonard's family nickname.

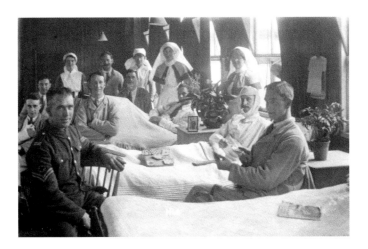

At the end of the War, Violet travelled to Iraq in what was usually called Mesopotamia, the area between the Tigris and Euphrates river systems, becoming a staff nurse at the 3rd British General Hospital (Military) in Basrah, a city more recently known as Basra without an h. The Turks who had once been in charge during the Ottoman Empire were at this time thinking about the formation of a modern republic in Anatolia, and the British and French were thinking about where to draw new borderlines for their own advantage in the Arab territories. She travelled to Baghdad, Mosul in Kurdistan and Kerind, about sixty miles east of Baghdad in Persia, where the British were constructing a new road through the Asadabad Pass. Evidence for this period can be found in an album entitled 'Kodak' which contains a number of fascinating, tiny, blurry brown snapshots which show (on close examination) street markets, bazaars, masses of troops, tents in a cantonment, palm trees, a military funeral, smooth-domed mosques – and one of a certain Lieutenant Rooke back in England. There is also a view of a Sikh temple with a notice outside it in English, a reminder perhaps that the Mesopotamia Campaign had involved the Indian Army more than the British Army. The Indian Expeditionary Force D in Mesopotamia had been under the command of Lieutenant-General Sir John Nixon, and was first tasked with guarding British oil installations in and around Basra. Later, the force served under the command of Major General Barrett and then under Major General Townshend, with whom they were at the infamous Siege of Kut. One of the photographs shows an indistinct group of people at Kut-al-Amara in 1921, with the caption 'Site of siege of General Townshend by the Turks'.

A scrap of paper in the album reads 'The Commandant and Officers of the Base Remount Depot, Tancoma, request the company of Miss Towers at a dance – 1 Jan 21 at 9pm'. She managed to attend Basra Races too. A booklet is included for the 'First Autumn Meeting 1920', priced at one rupee, which includes pencil marks showing that small stakes of two or three rupees were put on horses in several races. She is pictured with a Major Le Strange, the British Consul General in Kerind, who might have been the same person as the linguist and geographer Guy Le Strange who wrote *The Lands of the Eastern Caliphate: Mesopotamia, Persia, and Central Asia*. In this picture, Violet's hand is "in splint due to complication after sandfly fever". She is seen again, with friends, on board the King Frederick Augustus, a ship captured from the Germans, on the Shatt-al-Arab, the river near Basra formed by the confluence of the Tigris and the Euphrates. Violet was struck down by 'catarrhal jaundice' (hepatitis) in late 1921, which caused her to leave for treatment in India. A communiqué reads "Staff Nurse V T Towers arrived at Bombay January 7th (1922) was sent to Colaba War Hospital". This is followed by a message headed Eastern Telegraph Co Ltd which reads, "Sister Violet Towers passenger on SS Huntsgreen P Said Delighted darling you so near welcome home Leonard and mother". She met them at Southampton on 6 March, 1922.

Colaba War Hospital

Leonard and Violet were married on 23 December 1922 at the Evangelical Protestants Hall in Worthing. They moved to Tilford, near Farnham, Surrey, and raised a family of three children. Leonard walked with a pronounced limp and suffered from recurring pain and cramp in both legs after his discharge in 1919, often using two sticks, but he was able to ride one of his beloved horses whenever possible, was a member of the Chiddingfold and Ledbury Hunt and President of the Tilford Pony Club and Gymkhana until his death in 1950. Violet Rooke died in 1969. Both are buried in the churchyard of All Saints Church, Tilford.

(Photos by permission of Sarah Saunders-Davies)

STORIES FROM THE
WAR HOSPITAL

ROSLYN RUTHERFORD'S
LETTERS HOME

Roger Riordan, who lives in Melbourne, Australia, has put his extensive family history on the internet in uncommon detail. From his pages, I found that his mother had worked at Beckett Park in 1917, giving massage and electrical treatment. Her name was Roslyn Rutherford, born 1893 into a prosperous family in Murrumbidgerie, New South Wales. Her personal letters from Headingley to Australia are an invaluable source.

She dreamed of becoming a doctor, but could not do so 'for family reasons'. In 1914, desperate to contribute to the war effort before it ended, she came to the conclusion that the only qualification she could hope to get was a Diploma in Massage. After completing her studies in 1916, she eventually arrived in England in late May, 1917 and joined the Almeric Paget Military Massage Corps at Beckett Park. She stayed in lodgings at 18, Grimthorpe Terrace in Headingley.

Massage Corps members outside the main entrance

The Almeric Paget Military Massage Corps was a physiotherapy unit which had been formed in 1914 by Almeric Hugh Paget, Conservative MP for Cambridge and Baron Queenborough, together with his wife Pauline Payne Whitney, who had inherited a fortune from her uncle, one of the founders of the Standard Oil Company. The Corps grew rapidly from the moment it was accepted by the War Office, along with the increasing demand for physiotherapy, then known as 'Massage and Electrical Treatment', and in 1916 it became responsible for physiotherapy in all military hospitals and convalescent units. The Pagets and other private donors provided its funds until it received a government grant.

She wrote letters home frequently, beginning from the moment she arrived, in the knowledge that some of them would never reach their destination: she often wrote about things not arriving because they had been "subbed", in other words carried on a ship which had been sunk by a submarine. The letters, says her son, were written on poor quality paper, sometimes in ink, sometimes in pencil.

The full versions can be found online at www.corybas.com. The extracts here are all about her time at the 2nd Northern General, which she left in 1918, when she found that the Massage Corps was distinctly unimpressive. She joined the Scottish Women's Hospitals Auxiliary, a feminist group operating under the wing of the French Red Cross at a military hospital in picturesque Royaumont Abbey, which is near Asnières-sur-Oise, about twenty-five miles north of Paris. Today, it is often used as a film location, and Pink Floyd performed there in 1971.

All of the following letters to her mother were transcribed by her son, and most have her Grimthorpe Terrace address on the top. I have pruned them.

Dear Mother,   *2 June 17*

I am on my post at last, and jolly glad to back at work after so long. Leeds, at present, is quite a nice place…The trees are glorious, so huge and green. The hospital is in the center of a huge park, so huge in fact that although I live on the outskirts of it, I have about two miles to go to work. Fortunately a tram runs up quite close to it. I am in the electrical department and it fairly makes me weep to see how the poor devils are treated. There is such a shortage of masseuses that we simply fix up the batteries, of which we have about thirty, and let the men do themselves. They are pouring in all the time and we are kept busy taking the battery off one and putting it on the next. They use them as one might expect the poor ignorant things to do. It is dreadful.
My landlady is an old dear so far. She has three sons at the war and makes her own bread…
… It is so long since I have heard from Chappie I am afraid something must have happened to him… I think I will like this place immensely if it does not break my professional heart. I wish you could see the whole countryside a solid blot of yellow buttercups… Best love. R.

11 June 17

…I am quite happy here… I have a dear little Canadian boy, who is such a pet. He is only eighteen and was shot clean through the buttocks. One leg escaped scot free, but in the other the sciatic nerve was injured. He has been so unhappy, poor little beggar, because he can't stand on his good leg yet, so cannot have crutches. Today when I was doing him he moved his foot a fraction of an inch and he was so pleased his eyes filled with tears and he could not speak for quite a long time…
…The fields are a solid mass of gold with buttercups. I went out on Saturday and gathered a sheaf of them. They are glorious. Every lawn is white with daisies. They come up by the thousand every time the grass is cut…
I wish you could see the laburnum. It is perfectly beautiful. Headingley looks like the Wellington hills when the wattle is out. The last few days have been most beautifully warm, almost like our own days. There are swimming baths at the hospital but they are only open at 7.15 pm, and as yet it is a little bit cold for swimming at that hour, but I expect to patronise them later… Best love to all. R. X

14 June 17

This is a slack day, so I am putting in a few minutes in my domain writing while waiting for more men. The room has a glass side, and is in the full light of the sun, so imagine me quietly sizzling away… Most of the men are dears but more or less, mostly more, on the common side.
The hospital was once a University and one building is still kept for the students. The said students, mostly females, objected to the rude rough soldiers walking around their house, so a high barbed wire fence has been erected between their part and ours. This is [sketch] a rough plan of the buildings. You will notice the park, just on the other side of the road where the boys meet their girls as soon as they finish their treatment. Now this is a public park and is always full of men. They spend the whole day there. Since the students put up the fence the men have nearly four miles to walk to get into the park. Every night the wire is cut down, and do you blame them? I don't, my sympathies are entirely with the men, especially as the male students, who should be engaging in a

little war work, stand outside and jeer at the men for being put behind barbed wire. The men have threatened to kill them if they are not allowed access into the park and I wouldn't be a bit surprised if they did. I have inside information that it is our men who lead the wire cutting gangs…

We have several of the new Yankee doctors at the hospital. They are going to reform old England, teach them a thing or two and win the war off their own bats. They fairly make me sick…

Best love to all. R. X.O.

9 July 17

Aren't you glad I'm not in London when all these raids are going on? About thirty raiders flew over on Saturday, and I hear Oxford St. is devastated… Things seem to be going on as usual with not much hope of the end until after next winter, according to the men who are in France.

…On Saturday I went for my usual stroll into the country. We went to Ilkley, a pretty little place about twenty miles away. We trained to the edge of the moors, and then walked. It was perfectly glorious. The moors are a kind of plain, not nearly so cut up as the rest of the country and at present are covered with emerald bracken.

I don't see much hope of getting over to France for the winter but am still persevering…

Best love to you all. Roslyn XO

15 July 17

…You will be pleased to hear that I am under the age limit so cannot go over to France. The dirty dogs asked my age first then said why they wanted to know! Also the head masseuse said that I would not be able to go in any case as I was too useful and too great a help to her where I was. She thanked me for all I have done, and said she did not know what she should do without me, so as most of our moves depend on the head I see myself in Leeds in 1927.

I have had another promotion, another case of all honour, but no extra pay…

I am on the diathermy… It is a brand new invention and we are using it to experiment on the soldiers. If I take my hand off for half a second the man either gets burnt, or electrocuted, or something of the sort. And it stinks!

Best love to you all. Roslyn XO

12 August 17

…We have been visited by royalty this week. His Ex-Majesty Manuel of Portugal came round on Tuesday to see how things were going. He is a big man, hugely fat for one so young (28) and pasty… He had nothing to say to the men at all. Simply walked around discussing their cases with the Colonel, and flashing his big black eyes at Miss Axford. He is supposed to know something about medicine, and spends all his time, and the Red Cross's money, visiting the different orthopaedic hospitals in England. He had nothing to say to the paid staff, that means me!

I have not heard from the boys since the Big Push started so conclude they are all taking part in it. Things are looking very bad, and the boys at the hospital say it is much worse than the papers admit… Miss Stuart and I went off this afternoon to Roundhay Park, which is about five miles away… There are two natural lakes in it, but the people true to their English blood, have got the water nearly solid with papers, scraps, fruit skins, etc. The nicest lawns are also littered in the same manner! There are boats on the lake, but we did not venture on them…

Best love to all. Roslyn.

24 August 17

My Dear Mother, I do love you all, I've just got a huge bundle of letters, and all such interesting, entertaining ones too. I don't know how you heard that Chappie[1] was wounded, for I never heard a word of it. The dear little soul was killed in action on the 12th July. His Colonel wrote me a brief note telling me of his death. I am so very sorry, he was one of the finest men it has ever been my luck to meet. His, dear cheerful little letters have been the one link to home, that the subs never seemed to get. I don't know how I shall endure this foreign land without them. I am absolutely fed up with hospital… I have never met any women quite so two-faced, selfish, ignorant and quarrelsome as those in the Paget Corps…
Best love. Roslyn.

1. *Although Roslyn tells her mother in a later letter that she and Chappie were not engaged, there was an understanding between them, and she never really got over his loss.*

14 November 17

…I have just been to a Clara Butt concert. She is glorious. Elsa Stralia, an Australian was also singing. She has a most perfect voice, and a most pleasing one. It was an excellent concert altogether…
Bestest love. Roslyn.

19 November 17

…England is a dirty hole to live in. My hair is always a filthy mud color, and my brushes fairly make me sick, though I spend my life washing both. We have a new girl in our room, Irish, huge black eyes, black hair, small mouth and tiny face generally, and wears perpetually a far away expression. Ainsworth came to me and said "I do not like that new girl. Doesn't she make you feel as if you are in mourning? It makes me miserable to look at her." He is quite right too!
Bestest love. Roslyn

Bronte 26 January 18.

… The parcel arrived last Saturday amid much excitement and joy. Many, many thanks. It was the greatest delight to unpack it. Everything is beautiful and much appreciated including the little white boots with their pale blue pompoms. The cake was just too beautiful… There is a poor lonely Aussie here in the ward, and imagine his distress at not being able to eat a piece of cake made in Aussie! He can only take slops poured down a funnel into his neck. He is hardly disfigured at all fortunately for nature did not deal him a full hand to begin with. He comes from the West, Perth, has ginger-sandy hair, brick complexion, pale blue eyes and a thin, high, hot climate voice…
…We have been inspected today by the Major who runs the whole association. She is a hard faced citizen who looks as if she did herself well. We are having one or two rows daily with the housekeepers, the servants and each other, it is quite exciting and helps to break the monotony….
Best love to all. Roslyn

Bronte 11 February 18

…We have two dozen Yankee doctors here. They are jolly nice men too, and a damn sight nicer than the English to work for. The men prefer them too…

Bronte April 18

…Miss Barclay, the nicest person here, is going to Salonika next month and is going to get me into the same hospital if possible. She is leaving the Corps and going with the Scottish Womens Hospitals…

…The weather behaved as it always does for my holidays. We went out heavily booted and coated in spite of the rain. It did me good to see the sea again, even if it is only the tame North Sea. Redcar is the nearest point to Germany, and the driest spot in all the British Isles, notwithstanding which it never was fine for more than an hour at a time. On Saturday we took the train to Saltburn the next town (because people are no longer allowed to walk along the sands), and spent the day in the woods. We took our own lunch in a basket and after eating it we filled the basket with primroses. They were simply beautiful, but talk about picking violets! They are cut in the same spot. We walked up one bank and slipped back two. The mud was awful. We were covered from head to foot and sopping. Primroses prefer to grow on banks and have very short stalks, never more than four inches long and most of them about three or less. Next day I felt as if I had had a good hiding, I ached all over… Give my love to all those people who remember me. R.

Bronte 9 May 18

…I have such a warm back from learning some stunt swimming and sometimes it hurts…

You stand with your back to the water and your heels over the edge of the board then keeping absolutely still you just lean back. If you keep absolutely stiff, just bending your head as you near the water, you should enter first and it makes a bonzer wave. But if you bend at all!!! Well, I bent, so I should know…

The water is changed once a fortnight and nearly the whole staff use it, male and female, and all the training college students, too! It looks like cold black coffee, it is not really cold but has that greasy look on the top. One of the girls told a patient she was going swimming and said the water was hot. He said "But can't you get a hot bath in the hostel, Sister?"

…I am fed up with the Corps. They are an unbusinesslike crowd and have such a beastly secretary, all their members are dropping out…

Best love to you both. Roslyn.

c/o Dr Frews, Hospital Auxiliare 301, Royaumont,, Asnières-sur-Oise Seine-et-Oise, France

22 May 18

…I am putting my new address at the top for you to study, although I am still in Leeds.

…I am going up to London on Saturday for my seven days leave then for the big water! We sail at night so I shall go straight to bed and hope for the best. If I manage to get to sleep there is no reason why anything should happen of an unpleasant nature! Did I ever tell you I had to leave my picture show when the ship was screened? Last night I spent sorting my clothes and destroying letters, etc. It was an awful business. I did not get to bed till twelve so am now feeling like a boiled pudding…

(Photos by permission of Roger Riordan)

A BULLET IN THE HEART

Corporal Robert Martin Leyden of the Northumberland Fusiliers was struck by a shrapnel bullet in 1915, probably during the Second battle of Ypres. The bullet passed through his arm, chest and lung, and came to rest in a heart muscle, where it was discovered after an X-Ray examination. He spent time in several wartime hospitals, including Beckett Park, but in all of them it was considered too risky to remove the bullet by an operation. Cardiac surgery was in its infancy. By all appearances he appeared to be fit and strong, and the bullet was causing him 'little inconvenience' according to a report in the *Yorkshire Post*, so he was discharged from the army.

He resumed his prewar occupation as a linotype operator in Otley, skilled work he knew well: his father had worked in the printing industry and had brought the family down from Berwick-Upon-Tweed to Leeds because of it. At the age of twenty-five, and after working for a year, the bullet moved, causing him pain, so he was taken back into Beckett Park. Here he was visited by Sir Berkeley Moynihan, and agreed to an operation by him down at the infirmary. In the opinion of the staff, he was the best, probably the only surgeon available who could do such extremely delicate work. The new American surgeons who had arrived recently at Beckett Park were very interested, and later filled with admiration when they watched the successful operation by the great man. Robert would probably have been anaesthetised using the newly-introduced Shipway Apparatus, which delivered a continuous flow of anaesthetic vapour (a mix of ether and chloroform) through a tube inserted into the windpipe. The patient was sitting up in his bed the following day, the bullet extracted. For the newspapers, it was 'remarkable'.

Robert married Dorothy Leak, who was employed as a doffer in a worsted mill, at All Saints Church in Otley in August, 1918, and died at the age of eighty-two in Bridlington in 1974.

THE SHIPWAY APPARATUS

The Shipway Apparatus was invented by a leading anaesthesia specialist, the physician Sir Francis E Shipway, who believed that lung complications and falling body temperatures during surgery were caused by patients inhaling cold vapour, because when liquid anaesthetics vapourise, the temperature of the surrounding air is lowered. At that time, it was thought that by warming the vapour inhaled by the patient, both induction and recovery would occur more rapidly, which would lead to less anaesthetic being necessary. The apparatus includes a 'Boyle Bottle' ether vapouriser and a Junker chloroform vapouriser, each of which is held in a bath of warm water and connected up to a vacuum flask holding hot water, which has a thermometer attached to it. A hand pump was used to blow air first through the vapourisers and then through the vacuum flask on its way to the patient's lungs. Dr Shipway and many others thought that the technique was a great success because of the warmed vapour, but it was later found that this was due to the use of a long tube inserted into the windpipe.

The apparatus was put into use by the RAMC in 1916 and was still in military use in the Second World War.

• SHRAPNEL SHELLS •

Discontinued at the end of the Great War, shrapnel shells were artillery anti-personnel munitions which carried a large number of bullets, usually lead, which were ejected close to the target. Relying on a time fuse to disperse the bullets at some distance along the shell's trajectory, they were used mainly against enemy troops advancing in the open. They were also used in attempts to clear barbed wire entanglements, often with little or no effect.

AN IRISH NURSE

"All I've got for my grandmother are a couple of photos and just a little bit of information, but I do know that she worked as a nurse at Beckett Park," Mary Rose Everan told me on the phone from Ireland. A common story, but she had found more than many other family history researchers: Mary (known as 'Polly') Dunne was a Red Cross staff nurse who came to Britain to join the Territorial Nursing Force, trained in St Alban's along with her sisters Josephine and Kitty, and worked on the wards of the Second Northern General from 7 August 1917 until she left on 31 July 1919.

She came from a small rural village, but for some reason was allocated to the 'Derry 12' detachment, and in 1920 she was awarded the Royal Red Cross Medal (Second Class) when she was back in Ireland working at a military auxiliary hospital in Stillorgan, just outside Dublin, near Blackrock. She married in the same year, but died in childbirth four years later. And that is the sum total of the evidence, except for one mysterious studio portrait which may or may not have appeared in the press: Polly is seen with her hair hanging in plaits, wearing a costume and a jaunty hat which appear to be made of material printed with picture pages from the Daily Mirror. "It must have been for some kind of pageant," said Mary Rose. "It was taken around about 1920, perhaps in Watford, but there are no more details."

When Mary Rose visited England in the summer of 2013 with her son and her father, she took the opportunity to bring them to meet me and archivist Keith Rowntree and to look around some of the places, now on the Headingley Campus of Leeds Metropolitan University, where her grandmother had been nearly a century before. Keith showed us artefacts and the Sprittles scrapbook. We talked about what we were examining, and just a very little about general Irish involvement in the Great War, which is nowadays much less of a sensitive topic than it was after the experiences of the Twenties, when the Irish struggle for Home Rule was in full swing, and when the atrocities of the Black and Tans in Ireland could be measured against the atrocities of the Germans in Belgium.

TORPEDOED

Sophia Violet Barrett, known as Violet, joined a VAD nursing division at Carrickmines in County Dublin. In January, 1915, she was sent for duty to an auxiliary hospital for wounded officers in Monkstown. This was a private house donated by its owner. From there, she was transferred to England, to Beckett Park, where she stayed until April 1916, when she was sent to France. She was at No 6 General Hospital, Rouen until August 1918, and was mentioned in dispatches while she was there, in December 1917, which meant that she could wear two red stripes on her uniform. From August to October 1918 she was attached to No 2 Stationary Hospital in Abbeville, where she nursed wounded German prisoners, before coming home to Ireland.

On 10 October, Violet was returning to duty, on board a mail steamer, the RMS Leinster, when it left Carlisle Pier, Kingstown (now Dun Laoghaire), near Dublin for Holyhead in Wales. Most of the passengers were military personnel either returning home on leave or going on leave. There was a crew of 76 , 22 postal workers and 180 civilians – men, women and children. On the Western Front, the German army was being pushed back, the German fleet was on the point of mutiny, and on 4 October, Germany had asked President Woodrow Wilson for peace terms. The sea was rough.

Just before ten in the morning, about 16 miles out, a group of people on deck saw a torpedo approaching, which missed. Another torpedo struck the port side soon afterwards, blowing a hole in it. The Leinster attempted to return to Kingstown, turning 180 degrees. It was sinking slowly, and lifeboats were being launched, as another torpedo struck the starboard side, causing severe damage. The ship sank quickly, bow first. Violet was amongst the five hundred who died when the ship went down. Survivors, in lifeboats or clinging to rafts, were eventually rescued by the destroyers and other ships. The submarine responsible, UB-123, with a crew of 35, struck a mine in the North Sea eight days later and was lost, just under a month before the Armistice.

Violet's body was recovered and brought back to Carrickmines House, Foxrock. On 14 October, she was buried in Kilternan Churchyard, County Dublin.

• TOMMY AND TUPPENCE •

Tommy and Tuppence are two 'bright young thing' fictional detectives who appear in four novels by Agatha Christie. In the first of these, The Secret Adversary , which is set in 1919, they are introduced to the reader: Tommy Beresford, a recently demobilized soldier, meets Prudence ("Tuppence") Cowley, who served as a VAD. Both unemployed, they team up to form "The Young Adventurers Ltd".

HOT-TEMPERED, BUT DEDICATED

Sister Emily Violet Pratt, who appears in the Sprittles scrapbook, was born in Hallow, Worcestershire, in 1888, the third of the ten children of parents Henry and Edith. Before joining the TFNS as a staff nurse at Beckett Park, where she was known by friends as 'Violet', she worked at the Royal Salop Hospital in Shrewsbury and then became a massage nurse at Sheffield Royal Infirmary. She was feisty, possibly a trait inherited from her father, because a confidential report in her records at the National Archives describes her as "…an excellent nurse, energetic, methodical, self-reliant and very zealous. This latter qualification rather overrides her better judgement. She is impulsive and quick-tempered and not very tolerant of others failings. She has however improved in every way this last six months."

Violet's 1918 annual reports emphasise her capability, self-reliance and intelligence, but mention once again her "difficult temper". By 1919 she had matured into a staff nurse worthy of promotion: "She has done excellent work during the past years. For some time she was working in a ward specially set apart for certain orthopaedic conditions requiring great perseverance and tact and she was most successful in this department. She has taken Charge Sister's duties and would be very suitable for promotion. In her file is a letter recommending promotion for her and for Staff Nurses Misses D Alexander, M I Wright, M E Wilson and M Hanson.

Violet had agreed to stay on after the War for three months, but she was still at the hospital in February 1920, when Matron Mabel Whiffen and Principal Matron A Barneby signed her final confidential report in which she is described as "…a Staff Nurse who was promoted Sister in May last. She is a very capable nurse and above average. She is able to train those under her.

She is very zealous, energetic and self-reliant and has a high standard of duty. She maintains excellent discipline in the ward is very tactful with the patients is most professional. – She has not acted in a higher rank, but is capable of further responsibility."

Violet is standing in the middle at the back

Violet in later life

Violet was allowed to keep her TFNS badge when she was demobbed on 4 February 1920 because she had served for four years with good service. Her address is given as St Martin's Home, Cheltenham, and her home address as 178 Henwick Road, Worcester, not far from Hallow village. Her nephew David and his sister Betty recall that she seemed embarrassed that her family home was a pub and would write letters headed 'Royal Oak Farm'. This was not wholly inaccurate, because some agricultural land was attached to the pub. Violet was thought to consider herself a cut above village ways.

At some point, Violet befriended a disabled woman of a similar age to herself, whose father was wealthy and lived in Scotland in a grand house with servants. Violet went to live with them and was able to use her nursing skills to great effect, because her friend regained much of the use of her legs. When her friend's father died he left his estate jointly to his daughter and to Violet. Violet never married, and outlived her friend, dying in 1987 aged one hundred. She left all of her estate to charity.

(Thanks to Jacqueline Hartwright of the Hallow History Group for this information)

> Such cases (terrible facial injuries) existed in all the warring countries, as did the policy of isolation – for the most part voluntarily – in closed nursing homes. In France, 9,900 men with destroyed faces formed a special veterans' association after the war. (From *The Beauty and the Sorrow* by Peter Englund)

ANNIE STOREY'S SOUVENIRS

In the impressive Liddle Collection in the Brotherton Library of the University of Leeds, two box files contain books, a substantial scrapbook of mainly photographs and press clippings, medals and other items which belonged to Annie Storey, who worked at Beckett Park for the duration of the War. There is some doubt as to her exact status, because she is variously described as a VAD and as a Sister. I suspect that she was the 'M.Storey' who is listed in the *British Journal of Nursing* of 3 November 1917 as having been appointed as an assistant matron at the Second Northern General Hospital. This seems likely to me, partly because the BJN was not always well proofread and partly because several of the items in the collection are letters from King Manuel of Portugal, which are unlikely to have been seen by a VAD or an ordinary staff nurse. She was also in her late forties, having been born in 1870. It is hard, to say the least, to find any records, because before 1919 there was no register of nurses, and no national regulations for their training.

King Manuel was, in fact, an ex-king, who had lived in exile as a personal friend of King George V in the United Kingdom ever since the 1910 revolution, when the Portuguese First Republic was declared. He had escaped to Gibraltar on the royal yacht, narrowly avoiding an armed group which was in pursuit. During the Great War he was based in Fulwell Park, Twickenham, near London, and defended Portugal's entry into the conflict on the side of the Allies. He made himself available for the war effort, but was apparently disappointed when he was assigned a post in the British Red Cross. He put plenty of energy into visits to the front and to hospitals around the country, including Beckett Park. He is credited with the creation of the Orthopaedic Department at the Shepherd's Bush Military Hospital in London, which continued to function until 1925, dealing largely with war-related disfigurements, and he took a special interest in the orthopaedic aspects of Beckett Park Hospital: all of the letters which Annie Storey saved are to Major W A Stott, who was in charge of the rehabilitation programme. The letters are signed 'Manuel R'.

The first one, dated 10 June, 1918, is about an article that he intended to put together for Sir Robert Jones's book on orthopaedic surgery. "I have already had a long conversation with Sir Robert Jones on the subject," he writes, "and my article will be on the "scheme and organization of the curative workshops". I would be very grateful if you would let me know what you intend writing, as I think we ought to try to divide our task and by this means avoid overlapping in our respective articles". He goes on to ask for particulars of what is going on in Leeds and wants examples of how the workshops have benefited the participants. In a letter sent from London on 17 June he asks Stott to send him photographs of the 'curative workshops' and tells him that he would like to discuss these further with him because he is writing an article on the subject. A letter of 27 June 1918, sent from the Hotel Majestic in Harrogate, informs Stott that he will postpone his visit because he has just heard about an outbreak of influenza. On 25 June 1919, he thanks Stott for the 'very valuable assistance' he has given, asks for further thanks to be given to the patients who have helped him, and encloses a copy of his final report for the Joint War Committee of the British Red Cross Society and Order of St John. A synopsis of this is clipped to the letter: the results of the workshops are divided into the categories of Physical, Psychological, Morale, Economical and Training. There are conclusions about the links between centres, and between military and civil life.

An extension ward. Annie is on the right.

Annie's books include *Animal Physiology* by E Tulley Newton (1878), which includes sections on human anatomy, the alimentary canal, the blood and the sensory organs, a pamphlet entitled *Helps to Worship* with "Annie Storey - in memory of her Confirmation April 8th 1888" in the flyleaf, and *The Vision Splendid,* by John Oxenham, which was published in 1917. John Oxenham was the pen-name of William Arthur Dunkerley, who was a prolific English journalist, novelist, hymn-writer and poet who became the mayor of Worthing in 1922. His *Bees in Amber: a little book of thoughtful verse,* had been a best-seller in 1913. The foreword to *The Vision Splendid* is like a sermon: "Is the outcome of this latest world tragedy to be loss or gain? Under God, it rests with ourselves. The greatest world tragedy of all ended on the Cross… the one great loss to the world so far is the loss of the German soul… if this fierce flame free us from the ruinous wastage of drink - from the cancer of immorality – from the shame of our housing systems both in town and country – and bring about a fairer apportionment of the necessities of life – a living wage to all workers, leisure to enjoy, and opportunities to possess and progress – it will have done very much."

In the scrapbook, a number of full-colour postcards, none with any writing on the back, depict in a series of caricatures relationships between Allied troops and Arabs in Alexandria, Egypt. This was a base for troops in the Mesopotamia Campaign, and where a number of military hospitals were situated. The figures in them, drawn by an Ottoman painter of Armenian descent, Vahram Manavian, all have spindly legs and the jellabiya-clad Arab men all wearing red fezzes on their heads: an officer asks a policeman the way to the Nouzha Gardens (famous zoological park), a sailor and a kilted Scotsman push their luck by inviting a woman in a chador to "Step this way, miss", a policeman holding two street urchins by the scruffs of their necks has the caption "Come to the Caracol" (police station), two officers are pestered by barefoot pedlars while a Jewish man with a black hat and a red beard looks on and holds up a cloth with the flags of the Allies on it, and an Australian in a bush hat is seen punching a man with shoe-shine gear in the face with the caption "Get out! Etla barra! Annie must have spoken to men who had been to Alexandria in one capacity or another, so did she hear about the events of 2 April (Good Friday) 1915, when an estimated 2500 drunken New Zealand and Australian troops rioted in the Haret Al Wassir red-light district of Cairo's Ezbekieh Quarter? The so-called 'Battle of the Wazzir' allegedly began as a reprisal for the spread of venereal disease and was not helped by rumours that Egyptian pimps had stabbed soldiers. It became a milestone in the unofficial history of the Anzacs.

Embroidery in a Curative Workshop

Christmas 1915

The photographs of patients, staff and friends are often accompanied by names, but very few of them lead to records, except for some which show the dates the Victory or the Star medals were awarded. The patients in the indoor photographs, either in what can be assumed are the blue uniforms made for the wounded or in bed-shirts, are mostly from the wards in which Annie worked, or so I assume. The men in the iron-framed beds sit up if they can, sometimes with pipes of tobacco or cigarettes in their mouths, sometimes managing wan smiles. Typically, those able to stand and assorted nurses are arranged around them. There are wheelchairs, bandaged heads, arms in slings. Tables carry arrays of medicinal bottles of different sizes, enamel basins, jugs and ewers, vases of cut flowers, pots of hyacinths. Glimpses of ceiling plasterwork provide slight clues for anyone searching for the actual converted classroom in the main college building. Several photographs taken in the large huts in the grounds show the same ward with and without Christmas decorations made up of chrysanthemums, paper chains, holly sprigs and strings of little flags – Great Britain, Italy, France and Japan. The Matron-in-Chief, Miss Euphemia Steele Innes herself, faces the camera in one of them, sitting in a wicker chair. Annie herself appears in another. In a small room with a polished chest of drawers in the background, four patients are seen examining a length of embroidery, probably made in one of the curative workshops. Two photographs taken at Christmas in 1915 show several hundred staff and patients either standing or sitting at long tables, all crammed into a decorated main hall. One taken at the same time of year in 1916 shows what appears to be a staff dinner, with pudding on the plates.

Theo – a Belgian officer

On the high open terrace at the front of the main building, on a sunny Whit Monday (28 May 1917), a tea party took place, with broadly grinning patients holding enamel mugs accompanied by an orderly, Miss Morton, Miss Blockley, Miss Orwin and Nurse Robinson. The women with the 'Miss" were VAD nurses, or 'Vedettes'. At least one of the huts had an open veranda at its side, and there were little gardens near others. Patients seem to have worn regular uniforms in preference to the blue ones whenever they could, especially when outside, with shining boots and sparkling buttons accompanying the slings and pots. Twenty immaculately uniformed nurses sitting in deckchairs and on a lawn full of daisies holding cups and saucers is labeled 'Vedetts Otley 12th Home' and one or two other photographs seem to have been taken in the grounds on open days, with children and other civilians present.

The official group photographs seem to have been commissioned from someone with a superior lens. One shows Colonel Littlewood with six (unnamed) soldiers in Belgian uniform, three on each side, with a dozen RAMC sergeants formed up behind him on the main steps. There are individual portraits of exiled Belgians as well, including a striking one of a young officer in a studio, dangling a ceremonial sword from his belt, signed simply 'Theo'. The Belgians were assumed to be French-speaking in official communications, with little mention of Flemish. Any modern tourist in search of the landmarks of the Great War will find that the famously pulverised market town of Ypres is actually known as Ieper by the Flemish-speaking people who live there. The German occupiers of the country played up the differences and tensions between the country's two language groups, just as they did in the Second World War. The Belgians at Beckett Park wore a dark blue uniform similar in style to that worn by the French in the early part of the conflagration. Other individuals who appear in the scrapbook include a few patients who were either particularly memorable for Annie or who had a supply of studio portraits to give away – a kilted Sergeant Shaw, a smartly-suited J.W. Penrose carrying a trumpet, a blurry Corporal Stacker wearing his Australian bush hat with his hospital uniform, next to a large motor car outside the main entrance, Private Read, Lance-Corporal Dawson, F.Shires from the Royal Engineers… if the names Annie wrote sporadically next to the group photos were compiled into a list with these, it would provide years of work for someone trying to trace their descendants through appeals in the press and online. Two portraits of individual nurses stand out, one signed by Edith E Clough and one by Kathleen M E Whitaker.

The hospital entertainment was provided partly by the 'Cheero Boys', RAMC men who dressed as pierrots and who performed in a large hut provided by the YMCA. Annie was as impressed as anyone else at Beckett Park by these, devoting a page to two photographs, one of them embellished with tinting ink. The performers are named in the margin – 'Sgt Beck, Sammy Lindsey, Fryer, Fenton, Brown, Hartley, Rostron' – names which have disappeared into the mists with the rest. If only a script for one of the shows turned up! Annie may have had friends at the Royal Infirmary, Newcastle-Upon-Tyne and at the Leeds Township Infirmary (now St James's) because there are group photographs of doctors and nurses from these.

There is also a photograph of eight soldiers, all holding cigars, with 'German Wounded off Somme July 10-10-16' written underneath, one of them marked with an X. This is one of two intriguing items, the other being a complete booklet published by the Gemeinsames Zentralnachweisebureau (Central Bureau of Information) in Vienna in 1915. With the number 349 and 'Nachrichten über Verwündete und Kranke' (News of the Sick and Wounded) on the front, a title which is translated into the languages of the multicultural Austro-Hungarian Empire – Hungarian, Czech, Slovak, Ukrainian, Romanian, Slovenian and Croatian – the booklet provides alphabetical lists of the names of many hundreds of combatants. A scan of these suggests that, in this booklet at least, few of them had German as a first language: there are plenty of Schmidts and Müllers but even more with names like János Nagy (Hungarian) who was referred to a hospital in Budapest, or Wenzel Soukup (Czech) who ended up at one in Karlsbad in Bohemia, a town known a few years later as Karlovy Vary. So why did Annie have this and save it? Did she know any of the owners of the names, or is it just a curiosity? It certainly gives an insight into the make-up of the Central Powers troops who were usually known as 'the Germans' or 'the Hun'.

German wounded

She collected a number of newspaper clippings. One of these is about Corporal Robert Leyden, who was discharged with a shrapnel bullet still in a heart muscle, because it was thought at first to be too risky to remove it. His story is told separately. There is a full account of the visits of King George and Queen Mary from the *Yorkshire Post*, also featured separately, and a few paragraphs about Captain William Crymble of the RAMC, senior assistant medical officer at the Leeds Township Infirmary until 1914, who had been interned in Saxony after being captured in the first days of the War, then released in a prisoner exchange, and who died of enteric fever in Egypt on his way back from India. Other clippings date from 1920s, showing, for example, Canadians at the consecration of the huge memorial at Vimy Ridge. Annie pasted in written-out poems, some by patients dedicated to her ("There's a dainty military sister/ In a hospital not far from Leeds/ Who is doing her very utmost/ To comfort our soldiers' needs…"), some patriotic ("Trust to the boys in khaki,/ Trust to the boys in blue, / Trust to God All Mighty,/ To pull old England through") and some by popular poets of the time like Rudyard Kipling (*Lest We Forget*) and Lieutenant Colonel John McCrae, a Canadian doctor who wrote *In Flanders Fields,* which became much-memorised and recited after its publication in the London magazine *Punch* in December 1915.

She also kept her own record of patients who passed through the hospital in a rather startling series of pages entitled 'Remembrances'. These are ruled up and made to look like the pages in a visitor's book, with the following headings: Number, Rank, Regiment, Date when wounded, Place where wounded or sick, Engagements and What would you do with the Kaiser? The service numbers and names of men and regiments yield little more than medals when they are looked up, but there is some interesting information on the variety of sicknesses and wounds treated at Beckett Park, although many of the men wrote just 'Sick' or 'Wounded'. There are brief mentions of amputated arms and legs, chest wounds, septic poisoning, the effects of 'shell gas', trench feet, trench fever and pleurisy, to give a few examples. The list of engagements is a tour through the principal battles, with many mentions of Gallipoli or the Somme and a few of disasters at sea. The column under which men are invited to deal with the Kaiser contains a range of imaginative suggestions, ranging from the sadistic ("Make him eat pins", "Pull his nails out one by one") through the conventionally patriotic ("Leave him to John Bull") to the humorous ("Give him to some mill girls", "Throw him to the suffragettes").

A page of 'Remembrances'

Like others at the hospital, she kept an autograph book, which contains dozens of names of patients, who must in some cases have taken the book away for a few hours to complete drawings, cartoons and paintings. Subjects for these include Charlie Chaplin, "an old highlander", a girl in a kimono, Lord Kitchener and General Joffre, houses by a lake, a beach scene, the faces of pretty girls, a monocled man at a dance, a Dutchman in clogs, an Irishman carrying a pig, a shouting drill sergeant and the head of a horse. There are one or two 'propaganda pictures', for example a painting entitled A political and economic rapprochement' which shows a fat, brutal-looking German threatening a French woman holding a small child and one entitled 'The White Comrade' which shows Christ appearing to wounded soldiers. One of the drawings ("taken from a photograph") might have been by an American, because it is of the singer and dancer Hazel Dawn as she appeared in *The Little Café,* which played at the New Amsterdam Theatre on Broadway in 1913. She was a member of the original Ziegfeld Folllies, and was at one time the mascot of the US Military Academy at West Point.

There are artefacts in Annie's box too – medals for nursing and for the Junior Imperial Constitutional League (a forerunner of the Young Conservatives), and the belt she wore with her uniform.

PATIENTS

Private William Anderson was born in Gateshead in 1896, and received treatment in the Department for Treatment of Injuries to the Face and Jaws, or to be more concise, he was put into the Jaw Ward. He was a member of the Durham Light Infantry, and after discharge spent some time as an actor. His grandson Brian Anderson emailed an unusually sharp photo of a large group of men in patients' uniform sitting on the grass outside the James Graham Building, and told me what he knew in the course of a phone call:

"We don't know much about him really… although he was my grandfather my wife has done most of the research. He was in the Beckett Park Hospital because shrapnel blew some of his face away… I've see a postcard which he sent to his little brother from Doncaster, which show him with a group of his mates which he called 'The Scruffs'. He is turning his face in the photo so you can see just the good side.

He had a daughter called Irene Mary after he married in 1919 and she was named after one of the nurses. He had told her that he would continue to remember her that way, because she had cared for him so well.

He couldn't get a full time job after the War, and he took to drink, but we found him in a play. His photo was in a book from 1935 in the theatre. He was tied up with The Little Theatre in Gateshead, the only one to open in the Second World War. It was next to the Barrage Balloon Centre. His wife was a seamstress who made many costumes at home, then took them in.

In the photo he is in a group of guys with caps on, on the right hand side. He is the third one in. He died in 1967 in a home in Newcastle."

Further enquiries at the Little Theatre produced the following from Jim Race, Chairman of Progressive Players Gateshead Ltd: " It would appear that William was a member of the Progressive Players from 1933 to 1939. His first acting part was in *Great Expectations* in December 1933. This play was adapted from the Dickens novel by Hope Dodds. Hope was one of the founders of our company in 1920, along with her sisters Ruth and Sylvia. In Great Expectations, William played two small parts: a cavalry sergeant and a policeman. Following this, William's stage appearances for us were as follows:

> Inspector Japp in Agatha Christie's *Black Coffee,* in November 1934.
> Hartley in *A Romany Reaping* by Kathleen Close, January 1935. **
> Karl in *The Path Of Glory* by L Du Garde Peach, October 1935. **
> Major Belford in *The Deuce* Is In Him by George Colman, March 1937.
> Charles Wilson in *The Pitman's Pay* by Ruth Dodds, April 1937. **
> (This play was written in 1922 by our principle founder, Miss Ruth Dodds, and
> produced in 1922 and 1926. Its re-presentation in 1937 would probably have
> been a major event.
> An 'Irregular' in *Juno And The Paycock* by Sean O'Casey, December 1938.
> Ned White in In The Mist by Anthony Gittins, February 1939.

After this there is no further mention of William in any of our play records. Photographs were, at that time, rather uncommon. Of the productions mentioned above, only three have any photographs, and these are indicated in the list above by double-asterisks. You can find these pictures on our website. It is quite likely that William is the man at the right of the third (rather faded) picture from *The Pitman's Pay.* His character, Charles Wilson, was a government spy sent to the north-east to bring down the fledging union of miners being set up by Thomas Hepburn.

Unfortunately I can offer you no real information about his wife. In those days, our wardrobe workers generally went uncredited in our play programmes!

Second Lieutenant John William Bateman has a story which is told separately.

Private Robert Bass has a story which is told separately.

Private Albert Clapham was probably at Beckett Park in 1918 and definitely at East Leeds Hospital in 1917. I visited his son Keith, now in his eighties, after he had got in touch after reading a piece about the hospital in *North Leeds Life.* Keith was eager to share his childhood memories: "In the Second World War when the blackout was in operation, I was about seven or eight. I remember the adults at Christmas when we were in the front room talking about the Great War. My father and two uncles were there – the third uncle had been killed on the Somme in 1916.

We were not a drinking family but at that time there was plenty of beer and 'gin and it' with a cherry in it which helped them to reminisce. My father told us that he had been at Beckett Park and

East Leeds hospitals because he had been gassed, but it can't have been that serious because he was fit. I thought of what he said years later, when I was doing my national service in the RAF, when we were deliberately exposed to gas 'just so you know what it's like' in controlled conditions. We had to take our respirators off – you hadn't to call them gas masks – for a few seconds and this sent all the lads stumbling about, coughing and sneezing.

When we walked in the country he used to mention the importance of looking after your feet, telling me that he had marched down these endless straight roads in France when it was red hot and they were thirsty – and the NCOs had just told them to suck a pebble…"

Albert Clapham's records do exist, I discovered, but they seem to be incomplete. He was born 1888 in Dow Place, Hunslet, son of a labourer. He enlisted in December 1915, his occupation given as clerk. The following year, in September, he married Esther Mary Swales, a fact which came as news to Keith, because his father had never mentioned it. He got married for the second time in 1932, to Keith's mother Sarah.

He was at various stages of the War with the West Yorkshire Regiment, the Durham Light Infantry, the Royal Fusiliers and the Royal West Kent Regiment, so it is difficult to find the battles he was involved with, but in January and February 1917, he suffered from what were repeatedly described simply as 'ulcers' on foot, hand and ankle, which were serious enough to be treated at the General Hospital in Wimereux, and later at East Leeds War Hospital, where he stayed for three weeks. He may well have suffered from trench foot, a very common condition caused by wet and muddy conditions over a period of time, and part of his treatment could have taken place at Beckett Park. He received a leg wound in March 1918, receiving treatment at General Hospitals in Rouen and Trouville, and was discharged from the Army in February 1919. There is no mention of gas. Without the full records, it is hard to tell what really happened.

Private William Clark was born 1895 in Bridlington, son of a master mariner. He enlisted, aged seventeen, in the Bridlington Company of the 5th Battalion of the (Territorial) Yorkshire Regiment in May 1912, which involved training for two nights a week at a local drill hall and attending an annual brigade camp in Redcar, North Yorkshire. In March 1913, he moved with his mother, brother and sisters to Hull, where his mother intended to run a shop selling sweets and tobacco at 52 Bean Street. He was working as a shunter for the London and North Eastern Railway Company. His father at this time was a patient in East Riding Mental Asylum at Walkington, East Yorkshire, after being admitted for the third time in June 1911 and eventually dying there in October 1953.

On 4 August 1914, the 5th Battalion were at a camp at Deganwy, North Wales. They received the order to join the mobilization, and were soon at another camp in Darlington, moving from there to Newcastle to link up with the whole of the Northumbrian Division. William would have been occupied with 'home defence' and intensive training, especially after December 1914 when battlecruisers from the Imperial German Navy caused public outrage by bombarding Scarborough, Hartlepool and Whitby. All training was done in full marching order, with full pack and haversack, one hundred and twenty rounds of ammunition in pouches, full water bottle, rifle and bayonet and entrenching tool blade hanging in its case beneath the pack with its handle strapped alongside the bayonet scabbard. On 22 April, 1915, the 5th Battalion was thrown into action at the Second Battle of Ypres just about as soon as they had reached their billets from England, facing the threat of poison gas. William stayed in and around the Ypres salient until August 1916, when the 5th Battalion was transferred to Martinpuich on the Somme in preparation for the Battle of Fler-de-Courcelette. It was during the battle of Morval on 27 September 1916 that he was wounded. He had written to his Aunt Lucy on Saturday the 23 of September saying that he was "in the pink". His mother received a Field Service Postcard on the 4 October, telling her that he was a casualty.

From the beginning of April 1917 to 16 May 1917 he was in ward B1 at Beckett Park, and was discharged from the Army soon afterwards with five shillings a week pension due to wounds. He returned to 52 Bean Street, but his behaviour towards his mother became violent, and she eventually turned him out.

By 1924, he was appearing in the local press. *The Hull Daily Mail* (22 December 1924) carried a story headlined "Hull Man Who Broke Window of Mother's Shop" : "For willfully damaging a pane of glass in the window of a shop, 52, Bean Street, the property of Florence Clark, his mother, William Clark (30) , a pensioner, of no fixed abode, was fined 5s and ordered to pay the damage, £1."

Florence Clark's shop

Prisoner's mother said that she had to turn him away from home because of his violence towards her. On December 13th, she said, he came kicking at the front door, shouting to be admitted. Shortly afterwards she heard the window break, and discovered that he had put his hand through it. When taken to the infirmary to have his hand attended to, he said " It must have been my unlucky day."

William was admitted to the Hull City Mental Hospital in Willerby, where he died on 17 December 1928 of 'exhaustion from mania'. He is buried in Western Cemetery, Hull, with his mother and with his brother Tom, who had died of war wounds at home on 24 April 1923

Private James Clay, born 1894 in Little Preston, was a twenty year-old miner living with his parents Samuel and Anna in Queen Street, Woodlesford when he joined the RAMC in Garforth on 12 August 1914. He was attached to the staff at Beckett Park as a medical orderly. In September 1915, he became part of the Mediterranean Expeditionary Force as part of 33rd Field Ambulance, serving at Gallipoli and then in Italy as part of 89th Field Ambulance. The following year he was sent to France, disembarking at Marseilles on 27 October 1916. He was awarded a Good Conduct Badge on 12 August 1916. On 20 May 1917, during the Arras Offensive, he was killed in action. He is buried in the Faubourg d'Amiens Cemetery, Arras.

Private George Edward Clayton was born in Batley, and had just started his own tailoring business when he enlisted in the Leeds Pals September 1914. He survived the first day of the Battle of the Somme, and went on to earn a Military Medal, but on 3 May 1917 he was badly wounded in both legs at Gavrelle. He was sent back to England. After treatment in several hospitals, narrowly avoiding amputations, he ended up at Beckett Park on 11 October 1917. He was discharged from the Army on 31 December 1917. He died in 1971, aged 80, and was still having shrapnel removed from his legs as late as 1960.

Private J Crockett is listed as being in the 2nd Northern General Hospital with a GSW (gunshot wound) to his left leg in the Otago Daily Times (South Island, New Zealand) for 26 August 1916.

Private Josaphat Delisle served with the 3rd Pioneer Battalion with the Canadian Expeditionary Forces. He was born on April 3, 1891 in Valleyfield, Quebec. Before joining the 41st Battalion Canadiens Francais in September 1915, he had been a car mechanic. He was transferred to the 3rd Canadian Pioneer Battalion on 19 February 1916, landing in France three weeks later, on 9 March. Struck by shrapnel in the right elbow on 18 March at Ypres, he was transferred to No 1 Casualty Clearing Station the same day. The shrapnel was removed at No. 2 Canadian Stationary Hospital the following day.

On 27 March, he was invalided to England aboard the Hospital Ship Cambria, where he was transferred to King George's Hospital in London, then to the Canadian Casualty Assembly Centre at Folkestone on 4 April. He was sent to the Grand Duchess George of Russia Hospital in Harrogate on 3 May where he was to spend the next five months, before being transferred again, this time to Beckett Park on 15 October, for an additional month's hospitalization. He was subsequently transferred to the Canadian Convalescent Hospital, Woodcote Park at Epsom on November 16, 1916.

In his Medical Report of an Invalid, dated 9 December 1916 at Epsom, it is confirmed that he was injured at Ypres on '17.3.16 (when) shrapnel struck him on right elbow, shattering the joint, and that he was 'wounded on active service in the presence of the enemy'. It was recommended that he be invalided to Canada, his general health declared to be 'good'… 'Elbow solidly fixed at right angles…" He was discharged December 19th and placed on command to the Canadian Convalescent Depot at Hastings on 22 December. He was 'struck off strength' for Canada, on 13 January 1917. Three days later, he embarked on the S.S. Northland at Liverpool. (Information from www.camc.wordpress.com)

Private C Drummond is listed as being in the 2nd Northern General Hospital with a fractured tibia in the Otago Daily Times (South Island, New Zealand) for 26 August 1916.

Private Richard England's daughter, Vicki Warwick, has a folder of photographs and other items connected with her father, who was a patient at Beckett Park. She told me on the phone that she had read about the wartime hospital project in the *Yorkshire Post*, and that I could read all about her father on a website about the Great War for teachers, called 'My Learning'. After looking this up, I travelled to see her and husband Alan in Wakefield.

Richard was born in 1897 in Pontefract. According to the 1911 census, he was working in a sawmill when he was just under fourteen years old, living at North Baileygate with his older sisters Emily and Clara and his younger brother Charlie. His father had died. When he enlisted in 1915 he was still living with them. He joined the Royal Army Medical Corps, trained in Nottingham, and was sent to France. Like most soldiers, he sent postcards and letters home, in which he told as much as he could about the conditions near the front. He mentioned to his mother once that it was too cold to write, and was wary of the fact that a censoring officer would read everything, though he did include a few place names, which were deleted. He asked the family to post him things like writing paper, pencils and a battery for a flash lamp, but these did not always arrive, so he told his mother at one point to stop sending parcels for a while.

Richard England is on our left

The official telegram came in April 1918. His mother Hannah read that he had been seriously wounded. "He was hit by shrapnel in his back and buttocks," his daughter told me as she showed me a pale brown photo of Hawke Ward, which was in one of the many huts at Beckett Park. "He is sat on a chair by one of the beds. He was at that hospital under treatment until 1920." He had been transferred from Colchester Military Hospital, where his mother first visited him in May 1918, traveling by train at half the usual fare. As Beckett Park he would have not only received medical care but would have been a participant in one of the various curative workshops aimed at rehabilitation. He walked with a limp and wore a caliper for the rest of his life, but this did not stop him from owning a motorcycle and becoming a prominent member of the Pontefract and District Motor Club in the years following his discharge from the Army. He never talked much about the War.

Neatly stored in the folder devoted to Richard England are a few fascinating photos which give evidence of some of the shows he may have watched. A couple of these are of a pierrot group, but it is not the one which was based at Beckett Park, the Cheero Boys. I suspect it was made up of RAMC men at Colchester, because the white-faced entertainers wear sashes and have amongst them one man with a blacked-up face. Another photo shows the cast of what appears to be a production of Gilbert and Sullivan's comic opera *Trial by Jury*, or more likely a burlesque version of it. The entertainments, of course, were part of the treatment.

Lance Corporal Albert Harris, born 1893 in Harlaxton, enlisted into the 8th Lincolnshire Regiment in September 1914. The following report was in the *Grantham Journal* on 5 May 1917:

"The many friends of Albert Harris will be grieved to hear that he has been dangerously wounded. His Parents Mr and Mrs Alfred Harris of Harlaxton received a telegram on Friday April 27th followed by a letter regretting to report that L/Cpl Harris had sustained a serious gun shot wound in the right shoulder.

On Tuesday last they received a letter from France stating that their son was in hospital. Cpl. Harris was well known in Harlaxton where his whole life had been passed. On the outbreak of war he joined the Lincolns and proceeded abroad in Sept. 1915, remaining with his Battalion until the present time with the exception of one short period of leave in February 1916. Many impressions of regret had been received, together with sincere wishes for a speedy recovery and return amongst us. As one of his 'pals' (himself home on leave after being wounded a few months ago) says 'Albert Harris is the finest chap in the British Army, he helped me through many a tight place'. This opinion is endorsed by most of his fellow villagers."

The evidence that he was a patient at the hospital is a standard army form with a report on the result of an X-Ray examination, dated 24 February 1918 and signed by Captain Alfred Gough. The report states that as the result of a gunshot wound, the upper third of the humerus appears to have disappeared entirely. His grandson Michael, who sent this to the wartime hospital project, seems to recall that he mentioned being wounded at Arras.

He returned to Harlaxton after discharge and went to work for the Air Ministry as a civilian, in spite of his disability. He cycled five miles to work every day at Harlaxton and Spitalgate Aerodromes, in all weathers, until he retired in 1958, when he was awarded the Imperial Service medal. He died in Grantham in 1978, aged 85.

Private Matthew Henry Hart was one of a number of soldiers wounded on the Gallipoli peninsula who arrived at Beckett Park in the second half of 1915. Amongst the photos collected by Nurse Annie Storey for her scrapbook is one of him holding a violin, his cap on the plaster balustrade he is standing by in a studio. Born 1897 in Coddington, he enlisted at Market Rasen in the Lincolnshire Regiment, part of Kitchener's New Army, which joined 11th (Northern) Division. In April 1915 Matthew took part in final training at Frensham, then sailed from Liverpool for Gallipoli at the end of June, stopping at the Greek island of Mudros on the way. The division landed near Lala Baba, a hill one hundred and sixty feet high, at Suvla Bay on 7 August, and was joined by two Irish brigades. He was part of the first major offensive operation by formations of Kitchener's Army, which aimed to turn Suvla Bay into a secure base and to break the deadlock in the fighting with the Turks and their German advisers.

The high ground had to be captured, but the commander of the operation was sixty-one year-old Lieutenant General Sir Frederick Stopford, a man with an aristocratic background who had never commanded men in battle before. He was supposed to have retired in 1909, and had been given a ceremonial post as Lieutenant of the Tower of London in 1914. When his troops began the attack, he directed operations from an offshore battleship.

German commander Liman von Sanders had received a warning from Berlin about a possible Allied attack in early August and had previously dispatched Turkish troops to protect the most likely targets. After the landing, British troops quickly secured some of the hilly ground, but Stopford's inexperience and lack of energy allowed time for von Sanders to send reinforcements to take back what had been lost. There were more than 12,000 Allied casualties. Matthew was wounded at the beginning, soon after landing.

He died at Beckett Park on 9 December and was buried at Market Rasen three days later. On his black-edged commemorative card are two verses, which would probably have appeared on many similar ones:

> *A kind son he has been,*
> *Many troubles has he seen;*
> *When on earth he did his best,*
> *And now his soul has gone to rest.*
>
> *He was always kind and very good,*
> *And would do a good turn where'er he could.*
> *He's done his turn as a hero should;*
> *For his King and Country he's shed his blood.*

Private Francis has a story which is told separately.

Corporal Robert Martin Leyden's story is in 'A bullet in the heart'.

Private George Marriott was in the 1st Tank Corps, and was sent home from the front with shrapnel still in his body after he was wounded. His grandson Allan found the website for the project and got in touch to give as many details as he could:

"I have come across your website and appeal for names of men who were treated in the 2nd Northern General hospital, but I'm not sure if the story of my grandfather is what you are looking for. His name was George Marriott , who lived in Camp Road Leeds and ran a dairy there… at some time in 1918 (his records appear not to exist) his tank was hit by a shell and he got shrapnel lodged behind his knee. He was patched up at a field hospital and sent home.

For a year he worked in the dairy, shuffling about on his bottom, then in the early part of 1920 he was taken into the hospital at Beckett Park and operated on to remove the shrapnel. Unfortunately, he developed septicaemia and died aged thirty-three in February of that year. He left a widow and two sons aged four years and four months. That is all we know."

Private Fred Marshall was a painter and decorator from Tadcaster who enlisted in 2/8 West Yorkshire Regiment on 31 August 1916 at the age of twenty. He was married to Alice, and had one child, Cyril, who became the father of Robert Marshall, who contacted me after he had read a shortened version of the Dorothy Wilkinson story in the Yorkshire Evening Post.

He wrote: "Fred (*not* Frederick) was later Private 245118 with the 5th Durham Light Infantry and from 27 April 1917 he had been shipped back home and was taken to the Second Northern General Hospital at Beckett Park, Leeds, eventually to be discharged from the Army on 3 May 1918 as 'no longer fit for military service'.

His disability was described as 'Hysteria, Paralytic' and 'neither caused nor aggravated by military service' (!). Army forms also describe his military character as 'good, sober and honest' and in respect of his military service he was awarded a Silver War Badge and certificate, along with the British War Medal and Victory Medal. A family group photo was taken during this period showing his arm in a sling.

His 'Transfer Statement of Clothing and Necessaries' form for the return of Army issue, issued 4 May 1918, has the hospital stamp on it, and Army Form W3202 "Notification that a Soldier has been sent home from Hospital to await Discharge' states that he proceeded on 3 May 1918 to his home, Oakleigh, Wetherby Road, Tadcaster and further indicates that 'he will provide his own civilian suit and overcoat. Fred returned to the family painting and decorating business – Joseph Marshall & Co Ltd – and continued to live in Tadcaster until his death in 1966 aged seventy."

Robert Marshall added: "Since writing I have realised that I have a little more information which suggests that before being taken to Beckett Park he was in hospital in Glasgow suffering from unspecified wounds, which might explain the bandaged arm in the second photo). This is from a *Yorkshire Evening Post* article on 1st June 1917 which was reporting the death in action of Fred's older brother William, who is commemorated on the war memorial in Tadcaster. I don't have the original article but it is quoted online as below:

'Mr and Mrs J Marshall of Kirkgate Tadcaster, have received intimation of the death in action in France on May 17th of their second son Gunner **William Marshall**, RFA (Royal Field Artillery) The Deceased was previously in partnership with his father and brother as painters decorators and plumbers. His youngest brother Private **Fred Marshall**, Durham Light Infantry, is in hospital at Glasgow suffering from wounds.'

An article in the Yorkshire Herald from 1916 tells that his other brother **Charles Herbert (Bert) Marshall,** a joiner at John Smith's Brewery in Tadcaster, was in the Sherwood Foresters from May 1915.

I have also checked with my Auntie (Fred's daughter) and she says that, contrary to what I believed, Fred did have consequent problems with his arm during his return to work, particularly so because, in addition to the efforts involved in painting and paperhanging, he was also a signwriter. She also confirms the 'shell shock' and the fact that it was never spoken about much in those days."

Lance-Corporal J Martin was a pupil of Truro School in Cornwall from 1895 – 1897. In 1914 he joined a Canadian Regiment, and was wounded on 15 September 1915. He died more than a year later at Beckett Park, on 1 October 1916, aged 36, following complications after a leg was amputated. He was buried in Penzance Cemetery with military honours.

Second Lieutenant William Metcalfe was brought up in Scarcroft near Leeds, the son of Catherine Metcalfe, a widow and the village postmistress. He was the great uncle of Christopher Gallagher, who supplied most of his details after seeing the project's website. In 1914 William joined the 10th Battalion York and Lancaster Regiment as a private and with them saw action at Loos in 1915 and on the first day of the Somme in 1916. He progressed through the ranks quite quickly and was selected for officer training in late 1916, being commissioned a second lieutenant in the Leeds Rifles (1/8 Battalion West Yorkshire Regiment) in 1917.

He took part in another major battle that year, the Third Battle of Ypres, and was wounded in the assault on Yetta Cottage. After recuperation, he returned to his unit, now merged with the 2/8 Battalion West Yorkshire Regiment to form the 8th Battalion. He was wounded again in the assault on Bois du Petit Champ, one of the preparatory actions to retaking Bligny Ridge during the Second Battle of the Marne, which earned the battalion the Croix de Guerre. His jaw was shattered and his inner ear ruptured by a bullet.

His first treatment in England was at the Third London General Hospital in Wandsworth, but he stayed there for just a short while, because the reputation for maxillofacial surgery at Beckett Park was well-known, and he was soon on the ambulance train for Leeds to become a patient on the 'jaw ward'.

Christopher Gallagher writes: "He is the taller of the two officers in the attached picture, which I suspect was taken at the Second Northern General Hospital as his lapel badge shows he is no longer with the 8th Battalion. He was transferred on discharge from the 3rd London to the 3rd Battalion West Yorkshire Regiment, but remained at home on sick leave."

Private Alfred Paul, born on the Dewsbury Road, was a draper's assistant when he joined the Leeds Pals in September 1914. He was seriously wounded in the Battle of the Somme on 1 July 1916 and was sent to Beckett Park. He died on 24 July, and is buried in Holbeck Cemetery. His brother Thomas, who had enlisted underage, was killed on 22 September 1916.

Private Harry George Payne was known to family and friends as 'Mike', and he was the great-uncle of Chris Payne, who read a request for information on Beckett Park in a WEA newsletter. He supplied most of the details. Mike was born 1888 in Peckham, London, and his military service started on 24 June 1916 when he was 27 years 8 months old. Because of the date that he entered the Army, it seems likely that he was a conscript. He was a plasterer, working for Telling Bros of South Bermondsey. He served in France with the 193rd Machine Gun Company, part of the re-formed London Division, which took part in the Battle of Arras, which took place in 1917 after the Germans had moved back to the heavily fortified Hindenburg Line. At some stage during this Mike received a bullet wound in the left knee from an accidental discharge.

War diary extracts include a reference (on 4 May 1917) to one man with an 'accidentally self-inflicted' wound, almost certainly a reference to Mike's injury. He was initially transferred to one of the Canadian general hospitals in France, then sent on to England. At Christmas 1917, Mike sent a Christmas card home, giving his address as 'Beckett Park Hospital, Leeds'. A description of the wounding is included in his military records:

'Soldier was drawing his revolver from his holster in order to clean it. A rag was wrapped around the trigger guard and just as it was drawn clear of the holster the weapon was fired, a bullet entering Pte Payne's left knee. Man was in performance of military duty but was to blame. To be returned to unit for trial if found fit for general service. Not desired that return to this country (*i.e. France*) should be expedited. Period (*next few words unclear but probably* 'that he will') be incapacitated doubtful'.

It therefore seems that there was some suspicion amongst Mike's commanding officers that the wound was possibly deliberately self-inflicted, which would have been a court-martial offence. It seems that Mike never returned to France, and his recuperation appears to have been a very long one, based on comments in letters written by Mike's brother in law, Charlie Payne. His records show that on 27 September 1918, he was transferred to the Army Service Corps (number M/404084) as a Learner Driver, and worked at Woolwich Dockyard. He was demobbed on 10 February 1919 and returned to his trade as a plasterer.

Private John Pearcy has a story which is told separately

Captain Clifford Crawshaw Pickles is included in the story of Dorothy Wilkinson.

Private Thomas Pilkington and Private Arthur Pilkington were both born in Holbeck. Thomas was working as a butcher, Arthur as a commercial clerk when they enlisted in early 1915. Both were married. Thomas, who had joined the Leeds Pals, was seriously wounded on I July 1916. He died at Beckett Park on 3 September. His brother Arthur was transferred to the Royal Engineers towards the end of the War and was discharged in 1919. Thomas is buried in Holbeck Cemetery.

Lieutenant Leonard Frank Rooke's story is told in 'Romance'.

Private George Victor Ross was born 1887 in Glasgow. When I visited his son Edwin, who lives in St Chad's Avenue, Headingley, he told me what he could about his father, and showed me a discharge certificate and a scroll with 'Infantry Record Office, Ireland Bridge, Dublin, 16th February 1920' stamped on the back. George had two brothers from Belfast who were in the same regiment, the North Irish Horse, which was a relatively small yeomanry unit of the Territorial Force, raised by the nobility in the aftermath of the Second Boer War. Along with the South Irish Horse, they were the first non-regular troops to land in France and see action as part of the British Expeditionary Force in 1914, but George would not be at the front until later in the War because he enlisted in Leeds in December 1915. At some stage, he transferred to the Royal Irish Fusiliers.

"He was wounded by shrapnel," said his son. "His right leg was amputated, and we know that he lay in a shell hole in No Man's Land for a couple of nights before being rescued. He had to have treatment for years, at Beckett Park and after that as an out-patient at the hospital in Chapel Allerton. Much of the treatment consisted of 'improving' his stump. He said the doctor compared it with cutting little bits off the end of a stick of rhubarb."

Sergeant George Robert Scott, born 1893 in Leeds, was manager and barman of the Three Horseshoes in Otley Road, Headingley before he enlisted in October 1914. His parents were the landlords. With the 2nd Battalion of the Scots Guards, he was posted to France on the first day of April, 1915. On leave in 1916, he married Emily Clark. The 2nd Battalion was part of the 3rd Guards Brigade and on 31st July 1917 it attacked on the opening day of the Third battle of Ypres to the left of the Ypres-Roulers Railway. Progress was difficult, as they were met with murderous machine gun fire from German blockhouses. It was probably during this action, for which he received the MM (Military Medal, awarded to other ranks for bravery), that George was badly injured by a gunshot wound to his right arm causing a compound fracture. He was invalided back to England on 5 August 1917 and remained at Beckett Park until 27 March 1918, one of the patients who would have been very close to home and family. Although he had limited movement in his right elbow, he was posted to the London Command Depot on 30 July 1918. His discharge from the Army came on 11 February 1919, but shortly afterwards, on 10 April, he was back again at Beckett Park as a patient On 11th Feb 1919 he was discharged from the army. On 10th April 1919 he was re-admitted to hospital at Becketts Park although his service record does not give any reason. His death certificate states that he died from malignant liver disease on 6 June. He is buried in Lawnswood Cemetery. Thanks to Andrew Walker for this research.

Private Thomas William Sedgwick was a steel plate shearer at Kirkstall Forge when he volunteered to join the Scots Guards in October 1914. His moustached face is in an oval under the flags of the Allies in a portrait photograph taken in a studio, which was sent by his grandson John, along with the information that his grandfather had been a patient. Thomas was born in Melsonby, Yorkshire, in 1877, fought at Ypres, Neuve Chapelle and Loos, and was seriously wounded when the Guards attacked Les Boeufs on 15 September 1916 as part of the ill-fated Somme offensive. He underwent treatment at Beckett Park and the Infirmary, and went through no less than twenty-one operations before he died on 28 August, 1929. He is buried in Hill Top Cemetery, Armley.

Private John Josiah Wood died at Beckett Park of chronic nephritis (inflammation of the kidneys) in 1925, a disease he had been carrying for seven years. The death took place at what was by this time The Ministry of Pensions Hospital, most of which was situated in the auxiliary hutted wards. His descendant John Wood got in touch to tell me that John Josiah Wood had suffered from gas poisoning during the War, and speculated that the renal failure, and the cerebral palsy in one of his children, could have been caused by exposure to phosgene gas. John Josiah was a resident of Woodhouse after the War, and worked as a 'boot operative'. I speculated that he could have learned his trade at Beckett Park. He is buried in Leeds General Cemetery (St George's Fields) in Woodhouse, which closed in 1969 and is now part of the campus of the University of Leeds.

Between six and seven million soldiers (Other Ranks and Non-Commissioned Officers) served with the British Army in the First World War. Each soldier's record of service was stored by the War Office when it was over. Unfortunately about sixty percent of these were irretrievably damaged or lost because of enemy bombing in 1940 during the Second World War.

About two million were saved, and are now stored at Kew in the National Archives. In addition, three quarters of a million records for soldiers who were discharged for medical reasons (illness or wounds) in the First World War survived the bomb damage. Some (but not many) of these relate to Beckett Park.

DOCTORS AND SURGEONS

In the magnificent entrance hall of the original Victorian part of the Leeds General Infirmary, along with the marble columns and statues on plinths is a painted wooden board with the names of the honorary surgeons who were busy in its operating theatres more than a century ago. A majority of the ones next to dates before 1918 were associated with Beckett Park: they are mentioned in various books and journals like the *British Medical Journal, Leeds in the Great War* (1923), *Munk's Roll* and online sources like *Plarr's Lives of the Fellows* (Royal College of Surgeons), but the details are surprisingly meagre. Surgeons who were not associated with the LGI also worked at Beckett Park, and orthopaedic surgeons from the United States arrived in 1917, who are mentioned separately. Most surgeons and many doctors held ranks in the RAMC years before 1914, in readiness for mobilization for what they were convinced would be an inevitable conflict with Germany in the future, though of course they did not realize how long it would last, or how catastrophic it would be. Certain details, like letters indicating qualifications (eg MD, FRCS etc), and full lists of publications, have been left out of this list, which is as complete as it could be just before publication.

Edward Walter Bain, known as "Bill" to his colleagues, was born in Illogan, Cornwall in 1877, his father a banker. After finishing his medical training at the University of London 1n 1902, he held a number of house appointments, and undertook postgraduate study in Vienna. On returning to London he became senior clinical assistant to the ear and throat Department of the London Hospital, and surgeon at the Royal Waterloo Hospital for Women and Children. He arrived at the Leeds General Infirmary in 1912, where he stayed for nearly thirty-five years as surgeon (ultimately senior surgeon) in the ear, nose and throat department – his specialism when he was an RAMC captain at Beckett Park. According to his obituary in the *British Medical Journal* (9 August 1958), "He was a careful and deliberate surgeon with a leaning towards conservatism. He had a most equable and calm temperament and nothing ever seemed to disturb or excite him. He was extremely kind and courteous to all patients." Although he had retired in 1937, he made himself available again when the Second World War started and remained in practice until 1947. His publications include *Papillomata of the Nasal Mucosa* (1934). When he finally retired, he lived in Arkendale, near Knaresborough.

Joseph Coy le Fleming Burrow was the captain in charge of electrical work at Beckett Park, so he must have come into contact at some time with Rosslyn Rutherford of the Almeric Paget Military Massage Corps. Born 1888 in Bowness, Windermere, the son of a gentleman farmer, he graduated from the University of Edinburgh in 1910, moving to Leeds after holding house appointments at the Edinburgh Royal Infirmary. He became medical registrar at the LGI and tutor in clinical medicine. He came to Beckett Park after spending some time from October 1915 with the North Midland Mounted Brigade Field Ambulance. After the war, his appointments included Chair of Clinical Medicine at the University of Leeds (1936 – 1939) and he was a consultant physician to the Ministry of Health during the Second World War. According to his biographical entry in the

Royal College of Physicians' Lives of the Fellows: He was a colourful character, always immaculately dressed, and with great charm. His ward teachings rarely started on time but were always worth waiting for. He had a racy form of teaching, illustrating points by referring to topical situations. But he always stressed the importance of careful clinical examination and observation, and he scorned the excessive use of the laboratory test or the unnecessary X-Ray examination. Some people would say that he was flamboyant in manner but he was a very kind person and sympathetic to students… He was one of the early owners of a Bentley which he drove with great panache. He hunted with the Bramham Moor and was very fond of riding. His publications include *Malignant Spheno-Occipital Chordoma* (1924) J. le F. Burrow and M. J. Stewart (1924). He died in 1967.

Hartley S Carter, who was born in Leeds in 1887, the son of a building contractor, and who had been resident medical officer at Leeds Public Dispensary, served for two years as a captain at Beckett Park, for a year in charge of the pathological and bacteriological laboratory. He also worked in the Neurological Department, because one of his special interests was causalgia, nowadays described as Complex Regional Pain Syndrome, a chronic systemic disease characterized by severe pain, swelling, and changes in the skin. CRPS is expected to worsen over time. It often initially affects an arm or a leg and often spreads throughout the body. Carter made many observations, and published an article in *The Journal of Neurology and Psychopathology* (May 1922) which is based on the personal examination of over one thousand individual cases of injuries to peripheral nerves. Most of his observations and findings are based on the work carried out at Beckett Park, which by 1922 was known as the Ministry of Pensions Hospital, Leeds, and where he had became a senior medical officer. Even to lay readers, the article gives a strong impression of the great suffering of some of the patients. Carter describes causalgia as "an intensely painful condition almost entirely limited to certain sensory areas of the median and sciatic nerve distributions, and caused by lesions of these nerves at points more or less distant from these areas, and characterized by local vasomotor disturbances and general hypersensitiveness of the nervous system: a painful vasomotor neurosis due to irritation of a mixed nerve. Most of the cases seen and on record have been due to gunshot wounds…" Carter also worked on scars, and published another article, with Captain A D E Shefford from the Department for Injuries to Face and Jaws, entitled *Notes on the use of ionization in the treatment of certain types of facial scars,* so he was probably acquainted with the case of Robert Bass, whose story is told in this book. Carter worked at Chapel Allerton Hospital after the war, then moved to Glasgow to join the public health laboratory. Pathology and bacteriology became his life work, and he made a special investigation of diphtheria in the city. In his obituary in the *British Medical Journal* (June 1959) are a few words which indicate his literary interests : "He wrote extensively on medical references in classical literature, contributions which were outstanding for their content and for their clear and concise phraseology". He was also the literary editor of Beckett Park's magazine The Blue Band from 1918 to 1920, and the driving force behind it.

James Alane Coupland. As an RAMC major, he was appointed in 1911 as the first Registrar at Beckett Park, a position he took up in 1914. He was born in Harrogate in 1879, the son of a pharmaceutical chemist, and was sent to school in London, the Royal Masonic Institution for Boys, Tottenham. He was awarded his MB from the University of London in 1902, and was married the same year to Mina Alice in Leeds. In 1911, according to the census, he was living at 16 Springfield Mount and was described as a consulting surgeon, presumably at the LGI. His medal card in the National Archives at Kew tells that he spent time in France in July 1915 in the 24th General Hospital, which was at Etaples, but there is no record of how long he was there.

His particular hospital was one of twenty in a vast encampment which was a training base, a depot for supplies and a detention centre for prisoners as well as a centre for the treatment of the sick and wounded. Coupland appears in a number of official-looking group photographs towards the end of the war at Beckett Park having returned from France in 1917 to take charge of the surgical work. He died in 1957.

Samuel Wilfrid Daw, born in 1875, was an orthopaedic surgeon who had qualified at the medical school of Guys Hospital, where he served as resident surgical officer. He settled in Leeds, first as surgical registrar, then as consulting orthopaedic surgeon to the General Infirmary and to the Leeds Education Committee and Public Health Department. As an RAMC captain, he joined the staff at Beckett Park on 29 August, 1914, and in the same year married Joan Humphreys. Publications include *Orthopaedic effects of gunshot wounds and their treatment,* with foreword by Sir Robert Jones (1919). He suffered for many years from rheumatoid arthritis, and died in 1944 at his home in Polegate, Sussex.

Joseph Faulkner Dobson was the main organising force behind the planning to transform Beckett Park from a training college into a military hospital, and was its first administrator. His father was a doctor at Thornville, Burley Road, Leeds, which was where he entered the world in February 1874. Educated at Sedburgh School and Leeds Medical School, he became a demonstrator of anatomy, then a house surgeon at the Infirmary. He was elected an assistant surgeon to the Infirmary in 1903, and married Minnie Millington in the same year. He was a full surgeon in 1913 and consulting surgeon on his retirement in 1923. He was administrator at Beckett Park for eighteen months before ill-health caused him to resign. He was replaced by Lieutenant-Colonel Harry Littlewood, who was enthusiastically complimentary about his organising abilities when he wrote in the second issue of *The Journal of the Leeds Territorial Hospitals* (December 1917): "The plans for the scheme (to transform the college into a hospital) had previously been worked out, and estimates for equipment and buildings earmarked by the permanent staff. The buildings earmarked were the higher grade school, the Albert Hall, and other buildings in the centre of the city. Lieutenant-Colonel Dobson with great foresight at once recognized these sites were impossible. He went to Headquarters in York, and told them that the training college at Beckett Park offered many advantages. The authorities in York were very difficult to persuade to make any alteration in the original plans, but Colonel Dobson pleaded with such forceful persistence that he carried his point, and to his genius we owe a great debt of gratitude… Lieutenant-Colonel Dobson, Major Coupland and Captain Sedgwick worked with untiring energy to arrange to equip the training college, a task beset with many difficulties, and I never cease to admire the manner in which they carried out their work." Dobson recovered sufficiently to go to France, taking charge of the surgical division of the General Hospital at St Omer. During his time there he received the news that his seventeen year-old daughter had died at school. He returned to civilian work in 1919, becoming Professor of Surgery at the University of Leeds after Lord Moynihan's retirement. He was a keen fisherman and an prominent Freemason, becoming Master of Zetland Lodge in Castle Grove, Headingley, in 1929. His publications include *Lymphatics of the tongue,* with J K Jamieson (1920). He died in 1934

Ethelbert Rest Flint is mentioned as 'Mr Flint' in the story of Francis Lewis and also in Corporal Cropper's Memories, but I have found no record showing that he was in the RAMC. He certainly contributed to the work at Beckett Park. He was born in Scarborough in 1880, and qualified from the Leeds School of Medicine in 1905. After further qualifications at the University of Leeds, he became house surgeon in the Leeds General Infirmary. He was engaged in general practice in Doncaster until 1911, when he returned to the Infirmary as resident casualty officer. After being admitted FRCS in 1912 he was resident surgical officer at the Infirmary, where he remained until 1919. During the war, because of the depletion of both honorary and resident surgical staffs by the demands of war service, Flint was called upon to do the major part of the work of the surgical side at the Infirmary, to which was added the care of two hundred military patients as the war continued. This means that from 1914 to 1919, he did an enormous amount of surgical work involving both day and night work with little respite. This earned him such affectionate respect from the residents, the nursing staff and the students that he was usually referred to by them as "Father'" Flint, a title which stuck to him for the rest of his career. In 1918, he married Alicia Bay Farrer. He held the chair of clinical surgery in the University of Leeds from 1934 – 1936. On reaching the age limit in 1940, he became an emeritus professor, but continued to take an active part in operations until the end of the Second World War. Publications include *Pre- and Post- Operative Management of Surgical Cases (British Medical Journal* July 1939). He died in 1956. In his obituary in the *British Medical Journal* (14 January 1956), 'HWS' wrote: "Flint was a surgeon in the true Leeds tradition, following in the footsteps of Mayo Robson, Littlewood and Moynihan, who all influenced him in a large measure. This was especially true of Moynihan, whose private assistant he was for a time… He quickly built up a reputation as a careful and rapid operating surgeon of great skill and dexterity…" Alan Forty was the captain and dental surgeon who assisted Captain Munby, the consulting surgeon in the department for the treatment of injuries to the jaws and face until he retired in 1917.

Alfred Gough, RAMC captain, was a Leeds surgeon (described as "brilliant" by Sister Louie Johnson in the recording of her interview kept at the Imperial War Museum) and the cofounder of the Association of Clinical Pathologists. One of his publications, dating from when he was at the Yorkshire Pathological Laboratory in 1924, was *The Nature of the Red Blood Corpuscle*

Sir Harold Graham–Hodgson was a radiologist at Beckett Park, posted there after he was wounded. Born in 1890 in Liverpool, son of a doctor, he was educated at St Edward's School,

Oxford and Clare College, Cambridge. At the outbreak of war he interrupted his medical training to serve in the army as a despatch rider, but before the end of 1914 he had been persuaded to return to complete his studies. Two years later he qualified with an MD from the University of Durham. He was wounded after going back to France as a Battalion Medical Officer. After demobilization he was a General Practitioner for a short while before devoting himself to radiology. He married Lady Rosa Dorothy G Hallam. In 1924, he became Director of the X-Ray Department of Kings College Hospital until 1934 when he held the same post at the Middlesex Hospital. He was called in to examine King George V during his illness and was subsequently appointed CVO. In his later years, he was President of the Radiology Section of the Royal Society of Medicine. He died in Berkshire in 1960. I found most of his details on the Christies auction website in connection with his medals (Star with bar, British War and Victory Medals, Coronation 1953) which were sold for a total of £196.

George Constable Hayes was born in South Yarra, Melbourne, Australia in 1869, the son of a mill owner. After graduating from the University of Melbourne, he came to England too train at Kings College Hospital. He served at Belgrave Children's Hospital in Kennington as a house surgeon and as medical officer at the Golden Square Throat Hospital, which is now the Royal National Throat and Ear Hospital in London. He performed many eye operations, mostly at East Leeds War Hospital. He retired to Cheltenham, where he died in 1944.

J K Jamieson was an RAMC major (and later Lieutenant-Colonel) who was Professor of Anatomy at the University of Leeds. He was Assistant Administrator at Beckett Park.

Robert Lawford Knaggs was in charge of sixty beds for sick officers. Born in Huddersfield in 1859, his father a doctor, he was admitted to Caius College, Cambridge in October 1876, was at Guy's Hospital in 1883, then returned to Yorkshire to become Ophthalmic Surgeon at Leeds Public Dispensary from 1890 -1902. He was at Leeds General Infirmary from 1902 to 1920, becoming senior consulting surgeon there, and was Professor of Surgery at Leeds University from 1909 to 1919. He is noted in the London Gazette (13 October 1908) as an officer with the rank of major, whose services would be available on mobilization, and he must have realized the full implications of this, because his brother Henry was already a Lieutenant-Colonel in the RAMC. His name appears on Leeds University's Roll of Honour at the entrance to the Brotherton Library. Amongst his many papers and publications is *Diseases of the Bone* (1926). After the war, he married twice, in 1926 and 1933, and died in Devon in April, 1945.

Charles Edward Ligertwood (pictured) replaced Harry Littlewood as Administrator in May, 1919. He was born in Aberdeen in 1873, son of an advocate who was Sheriff Clerk of Aberdeenshire, and received his MD in 1897 from Yorkshire College, Leeds, which was affiliated to Victoria University, Manchester. His thesis was *A Form of Alcoholic Cardiac Failure*. He entered the war as a Lieutenant-Colonel with the Imperial Light Horse in South West

Africa, from September 1914. The Germans in what is now called Namibia were considered to be a military threat to South Africa's borders, and had a certain amount of support from disaffected Afrikaaners, so the conflict there must have seemed rather like a rerun of the Boer war. He transferred to the RAMC, and in 1916 he was with the 103rd Field Ambulance in France with the rank of major. He arrived at Beckett Park as a lieutenant-colonel when Littlewood finally retired, by which time the hospital was concerned mostly with orthopaedics and rehabilitation. He married Dorothy Craft in 1927, and for two years was Examining Surgeon under the Factories Act, 1937, for the District of Wivelscombe in Somerset. He died in Norwich in 1946.

Harry Littlewood thought, mistakenly, that he could look forward to a life of leisure on his small estate in Erpingham, Norfolk. Europe was at peace. At the age of fifty-two, he had retired from his work as a greatly respected surgeon in Leeds. He had become the Resident Surgical Officer at Leeds General Infirmary in 1886, and in 1896 had been promoted to the full staff and had charge of beds for seventeen years, after which he had been elected Consulting Surgeon. At the University of Leeds he had been successively Demonstrator of Surgical Pathology, Lecturer in Practical and Operative Surgery and finally Professor of Surgery. He had become well known for his dedication and hard work. Years later, Lord Moynihan was to write an appreciation in the *Yorkshire Post*: "As an operator he was safe. The rash adventure was foreign to his nature. He considered all aspects of a difficult case, and was hard to move when once he had reached a decision. He was cautious, but never timid; quick, without haste; full of resource in every emergency..."

When war broke out sixteen months later, he knew what he had to do, and was soon wearing the uniform of a Lieutenant-Colonel in the RAMC. He was put in charge of the Surgical Section at the newly-opened hospital at Beckett Park, working under one of his old students, now Colonel J F Dobson. He returned to a full schedule of operations, and when Dobson fell ill, he became the hospital administrator, a post he held until after the end of the war. Fredrick Cropper, an Orderly Room Corporal who lived in Macaulay hostel, remembered him well as being "very popular with patients and staff" and thought of him as a kind of squire, who every morning would walk along the long corridor between the hutted wards saying "Good morning" to everyone he encountered.

He was fierce, in 1915, in defending his belief that the war was entirely necessary. He delivered a rousing speech at a special meeting of the medical profession held in Wakefield which was reported in the *British Medical Journal* (25 September), in which he said, "What the Allies -and more particularly the British Empire - have to realise is that, if we are not successful, our fate will be infinitely worse than that of Belgium. They have been scourged with whips; we shall be scourged with scorpions. If the Germans once landed in this country, we should not waste our time discussing compulsory service - we should act, and be thankful if we had anyone to lead us to drive them out; but how little chance we should have if we were not prepared! Since the beginning of the war I have had large numbers of wounded men under my care - all brave and cheerful fellows.

I cannot imagine how any one seeing them and hearing their stories could delay one moment in striving to do all in his power to defeat any chances of Germanic domination."

He died soon after his second retirement started, suddenly, at Erpingham Lodge in December, 1921. At the time of his death he was Consulting Surgeon, not only to the Leeds General Infirmary, but also to the Victoria Hospital, Keighley, and External Examiner in Surgery at the National University of Ireland. He was, in addition, a Knight of Grace of the Order of St John of Jerusalem, which still exists today across the Commonwealth and in the USA "to prevent and relieve sickness and injury, and to act to enhance the health and well-being of people anywhere in the world."

W Maxwell Munby's specialism was maxillofacial surgery. He was the RAMC captain in charge of the Department for Treatment of Injuries to the Face and Jaws at Beckett Park, with Captains Alan Forty and A D Shefford to assist him as Dental Officers. This opened in May, 1916, with 150 beds. They were just three of the pioneers of reconstruction during the First World War, dealing with traumatised faces regularly – like that, for example of Private Robert Bass. For an article in *The British Journal of Surgery* (Volume 6, 1918), the three captains collected their notes on a series of cases and published their observations in *Notes on the Principles and Results of Treatment in 200 Cases of Injuries to the Face and Jaws.* Of the 200, 145 were admitted with definite injury to bone, and the remaining 55 were suffering from injuries to the soft parts only, giving rise to various disabilities. Other publications include *Mastoiditis and its Complication* by W. Maxwell Munby and R. E. Jowett (1926). According to *Leeds in the Great War* (1924), 'jaw cases' tended to be sent to the separate Allerton Hospital (57 beds), which was a large house lent by its owner for the duration of the war. Captain Munby was its Medical Officer and Mrs Harding Churton (Order of St John) its Commandant.

Alfred Richardson was a captain and a surgeon at Beckett Park , with a commission dated 3 January 1915. The son of a doctor, he was born in 1884 in Trowbridge, Wiltshire, and was educated at Epsom College and the Leeds Medical School. At Leeds General Infirmary he held in succession the posts of house surgeon, resident casualty officer, and resident surgical officer. In August 1913 he became surgical tutor and registrar. He married Muriel Gladys Smith in 1916, and died after an attack of coronary thrombosis in 1934. He is buried in Lawnswood Cemetery, Leeds.

Matthew Stewart was attached as a captain to the East Leeds staff, where he was in charge of cases of typhoid, dysentery and malaria. In 1918 became Professor of Pathology at Leeds University, a post he held until 1951. He gained a reputation as a highly knowledgeable morbid anatomist and histologist.

Walter Henry Maxwell Telling was an RAMC lieutenant-colonel who joined Sir Berkeley Moynihan to oversee Beckett Park in 1914. He was born in Surrey in 1874 and educated at Camberwell Grammar School, graduated from Guys Hospital, London in 1898 and was soon resident medical officer at Leeds General Infirmary. He was elected physician there in 1912. At Leeds University he became clinical lecturer on medicine in 1906 and lecturer in pharmacology and therapeutics in 1921. In 1932 he took the chair of forensic medicine, because acting as an expert witness in court cases had interested him greatly. According to *Munk's Roll* (Fellows 1826 – 1925) he became increasing interested in psychology in later life and also "deeply concerned himself with religion and ultimately identified himself with the 'Oxford Group'. His obituary in the *British Medical Journal* (14 May 1938) is detailed in its inclusion of his many interests outside medicine, which included freemasonry, the law, psychic research, opera, gardening and collecting fine porcelain. He was also "an excellent speaker, persuasive in argument, cogent in reasoning, lucid in exposition, and, when occasion demanded, delightfully and sparklingly humorous."

Walter Thompson, the son of a Wharfedale farmer, was educated at Leeds Medical School, and in Berlin, where he took lodgings with Sir Berkeley Moynihan, his lifelong friend. He became one of the foremost operating surgeons in Yorkshire, and at the time of his death he was Consulting Surgeon to the Leeds General Infirmary, Hon Consulting Surgeon to the Coronation Hospital, Ilkley, and to the Malton Cottage Hospital. He had also been Lecturer in the Practice of Surgery to the University of Leeds, and Hon Surgeon to the Leeds Public Dispensary and the Leeds Hospital for Women and Children. During the war, he spent a year with the medical services in Salonica, Greece, before returning to Leeds, and working at Beckett Park before becoming the leading figure at East Leeds War Hospital. He was not in the best of health himself, and became very ill in late 1923. His old friend Moynihan operated. He died at his house in Headingley in May 1924. Moynihan, in a moving eulogy (*British Medical Journal* 1924 i 937) wrote about his genius for friendship, his 'gravity of utterance' and his sanity of outlook: "..."I met him for the first time on the day I joined the Leeds School of Medicine....Our whole curriculum was passed together... I never knew an honester man....As a surgeon he was a fine example of the Leeds School. He was quite undemonstrative, cautious, exact, and safe. There was no display in anything he did. Every movement fulfilled its exact purpose. He showed the competence and the invaluable precision of the man who, sure of himself, is a master in the medium in which he works..."

Edmond Fauriel Trevelyan, born in 1859, occupied the chair of therapeutics at the new University of Leeds until 1909, and was one of the founders of the Leeds Sanatorium, acting as its physician. His principal interest was in pulmonary tuberculosis. He accepted the command of the 2nd Northern General Hospital (in the event of mobilization) when the Territorial Force was formed, but died in December 1911.

William Atkinson Stott was Leeds-born, and graduated from Yorkshire College in 1888 and was able eventually to add MRCS (Member of the Royal College of Surgeons) after his name. In 1892 he married his wife Martha at the church of St John the Evangelist in Leeds while he was living at Grove Terrace, Camp Road, Leeds, where he had a medical practice. From 1879 to 1883 he served as a trooper in the 2nd West Yorkshire Yeomanry, a forerunner of the Territorial Force, and went with the Royal Engineers to South Africa, sailing there in 1900, according to the London Times (21 February), described as a 'civil surgeon'. He was a captain in the 2nd West Yorkshire Royal Engineer Volunteers 1900 – 1901 (information from National Army Museum, which has twenty seven negatives photographed by him during the Boer War) and he was associated with them until 1920. His name appears on the Roll of Honour for the South African War, which is on a wall inside Leeds Town Hall. In December 1915 he was in France, where he stayed for a short while before he joined the Mediterranean Expeditionary Force, based in Egypt. In 1916, he was the officer in command of eighteen hundred troops on the transport ship SS Minnewaska when she struck a mine in Suda Bay, Crete. Fortunately, she was beached and there were no casualties. At Beckett Park he was a major, in charge of the Curative Workshops, and was visited by ex-King Manuel of Portugal there. After the war he became a Brevet Lieutenant Colonel. He is buried in Lawnswood Cemetery, Leeds.

Charles Wilfred Vining was born in Liverpool in 1883, educated at Doncaster Grammar School and at University College School, London. He graduated from St Mary's Hospital, London in 1907 with honours in medicine. Amongst his early appointments was one at the Paddington Green Children's Hospital. In Leeds, he established a consulting practice and became assistant physician and pathologist to the infirmary and lecturer in clinical medicine at the university. He was also the pathologist at Beckett Park from 1914, and when the new extension was opened in March, 1916 he was made medical officer in charge of cerebrospinal fever (meningitis) cases, tetanus and other infections in the whole of the West Riding area; these cases with their contacts were normally sent to the auxiliary hospital at Killingbeck. This is mentioned in Leeds in the Great War with the comment: "At times the work was very hard and exacting, but it was always done with enthusiasm and painstaking accuracy." In 1919, a medical children's unit was set up in the LGI, and Dr Vining gave up his adult beds to take charge of it: it was the first significant step in his path to becoming a leading paediatrician. He was the first Professor of Children's Diseases at Leeds University, and when the British Paediatric Association was founded in 1928, he joined as one of its first members. He often stressed that many childish ailments were due to mismanagement, and maintained that over-protection was just as often the cause of some behaviour troubles as was neglect. Parental attitude towards their young should be one of "observant negligence", he wrote, and the opening to his presidential address to the Leeds and West Riding Medico-Chirurgical Society in 1941 ran: " I will begin with what I believe to be the keystone of the whole of children's medicine, namely nutrition." Publications include *Rheumatic Infection in Childhood* (1925) He died in 1967.

G W Watson was the RAMC major who was Registrar from June 1915 to June 1919. He is described as 'Hon. Demonstrator' on the University of Leeds's Roll of Honour.

Arthur Longley Whitehead was an ophthalmic surgeon, born in Wellclose Place, Blackman Square, Leeds in 1868, his father a cloth manufacturer. He was a pupil at Leeds Grammar School and a student at Leeds Medical School, serving as house surgeon to Sir Arthur Mayo Robson at the Infirmary, eventually becoming surgeon in charge of the ophthalmic department, and lecturer on ophthalmology at the University of Leeds, positions he held until he resigned in 1920. Publications include *Ocular tuberculosis* (1922). He died in October, 1930 and is buried in the churchyard at Pool, near Leeds.

• CHLORODYNE •

Chlorodyne was a popular patent medicine with a minty taste which was available in local chemists' shops. Invented by Indian Army doctor John Collis Browne in the nineteenth century, its main ingredients were laudanum (opium dissolved in alcohol), tincture of cannabis and chloroform. The highly-addictive concoction was used to relieve pain, as a sedative and to treat diarrhoea. During the 1916 siege of Kut Al Amara by the Turks, some of the British and Indian soldiers living in conditions of starvation and disease who wanted to stay on their feet at any price kept themselves going on a mixture of castor oil and Chlorodyne. (From The Beauty and the Sorrow by Peter Englund)

THE ILLUSTRIOUS MOYNIHAN

"No training of the surgeon can be too arduous, no discipline too stern, and none of us may measure our devotion to our cause. For us an operation is an incident in the day's work, but for our patients it may be, and no doubt it often is, the sternest and most dreaded of all trials, for the mysteries of life and death surround it, and it must be faced alone."

Addresses on Surgical Subjects: **'The Approach to Surgery'**

Berkeley George Andrew Moynihan, then just a 'Sir', having been knighted in 1912, visited Beckett Park during the Great War whenever he could, which was probably not very often, because he was a figure of national importance who held the rank of Major in the Territorial RAMC when the War started (the commission dated from October, 1908) and Major General when he was demobilised in 1919. He was Chairman of the Army Advisory Board from 1916, and was active in France during the Battle of the Somme. He made a great impression in North America during a speaking tour on behalf of the British cause. He had a gift of oratory, was nothing like the stereotype of a reserved and self-deprecatory Englishman, and felt that he knew how the German mind worked, having spent some of his time as a student in Berlin, where he shared lodgings with Walter Thompson, who was also destined to become a well-known Yorkshire surgeon.

Today, a bust of the great man stands half-way up the main staircase which comes down to the entrance to the older, more ornate part of the Leeds General Infirmary, where he was elected assistant surgeon in 1896, and an oil painting hangs in its board room. He was surgeon there from 1906, and consulting surgeon from 1927 until his death in 1936. He was lecturer in surgery from 1896 to 1909, and from 1909 to 1927 he was professor of clinical surgery in the University of Leeds.

He had personal scalpels and other instruments specially made to fit his hands, and a bronze cast of them is in the Leeds Medical School's library, with a replica in the City Art Gallery. He is famous partly for introducing the use of rubber gloves in surgery, after studying American methods.

In 1909, he founded a small visiting club for surgeons who wanted to extend their knowledge, which travelled widely on the continent gathering information and first-hand knowledge of the latest methods and procedures at surgical centres. This became the Moynihan Chirurgical Club in 1929. At his own clinic he was an excellent showman for his work when visitors came, with a dramatic and engaging manner. He emphasised the necessity for the delicate and gentle handling of tissues by talking about "caressing" them, and considered every operation to be a kind of sacred rite during which the patient was surrendering his future or even his life to the judgement and manual skills of a previously unknown surgeon. Every detail had to be perfect, with nothing left to chance. Operations on the gall-bladder, the stomach, the spleen and 'short-circuiting' for duodenal ulcers were of special interest to him, featuring heavily in his extensive writings for medical journals, in which he displayed his elegance with words.

His visits to Beckett Park, though not accompanied by the parades and presentations connected with royalty, must have been special occasions: he was a tall, well-made man, retaining some of the striking red hair of his youth, who spoke with a soft voice. His humour was much appreciated and he was well-informed in painting, literature and music: on his tours abroad he found time to visit galleries and attend concerts. He operated personally on an unknown number of wounded soldiers, including Corporal Robert Leyden, who needed the remains of a lead shrapnel bullet extracted from a heart muscle. Any kind of heart operation was considered extremely risky in 1917, when he removed it successfully.

Some idea of his wartime attitudes and opinions may be had from *British Medicine in the War 1914 – 1917* which was published by the British Medical Association in 1917. The first article, by Moynihan, is entitled *The Institutes of Surgery*. His focus is historical, on the medical advances since the end of the previous century and on his view that the Germans were not the originators of most of them, in spite of Germany's "arrogant repetition of her claim to intellectual superiority over all nations." He informs the reader at the beginning that he was once a student in Germany, had lived with German students and had followed the work of German surgeons in several clinics, to strengthen his credibility and reinforce his patriotism. An array of facts, and supporting evidence selected from his encyclopaedic store of medical knowledge, follows. He begins by demolishing an argument which he had heard in Germany, that the introduction of the antiseptic system into practice was wholly to be attributed to German research, adoption and advocacy. He details how Joseph Lister, an Englishman, applied Louis Pasteur's advances in microbiology and pioneered the idea of sterile surgery, and how Lister always gave full credit to the French scientist: "A discovery is rarely the work of one mind. It is one observation added to another that makes the super-saturated solution from which the crystal of truth at last precipitates." In a section headed *An Appeal to Nature,* he presents his perspective on the history of medicine, mentioning Vesalius the anatomist, Harvey the physiologist, Morgagni the father of pathology and John Hunter, "who first changed surgery from a handicraft to an art based upon an accurate knowledge of diseased tissues, who first made of surgery a science." He goes on to include "Morton and Warren of Boston, and Simpson of Edinburgh, who, by the discovery of ether and of chloroform, robbed surgery of its agony and horror and made it accessible as well as possible." According to Moynihan, "Germany gave nothing".

He then moves on to a section entitled *Abdominal Surgery,* a topic on which he was the great authority. He gives a wealth of detail in relation to the removal of ovarian cysts, and how the nineteenth century surgeon Spencer Wells, "an old pupil of the Leeds Infirmary", had overcome all opposition to their surgical treatment "by his simplicity of character, his unwavering integrity, and his sweet reasonableness in argument". The history of operations on the gall bladder, the stomach, the brain and treatments for duodenal ulcers follow, punctuated at regular intervals by phrases like "arrogant Prussian fashion" and comments on how the Germans had contributed very little which was original: "The literature emitted by Germany upon the subject of gastric diseases is vast in quantity, prolix and turgid in style, lacking insight and interest, and almost utterly devoid of inspiration or original thought." Moynihan's angle on Germany was very much in tune with the official one, the prevailing Zeitgeist, as it were.

He became the first Baron of Leeds in 1929. A blue plaque to him was unveiled outside 33, Park Square, Leeds, by his grandson Dr W C Wynn Parry in January 2003.

• DEDICATED TO THE R.A.M.C. •

We called you the "Linseed Lancers,"
You men of the R.A.M.C.;
We looked upon you just as "wash-outs,"
The pets of old Maids and their tea.
We called you the "Poultice Dossers,"
And said you were safe from the lead,
Kept back from the line of battle,
Just tucking up fellows in bed.

R.A.M.C., Yes "Rob All My Comrades,"
We thought that a wonderful skit,
And, "Run Away Mother's Coming,"
We also thought that a good hit.
Your work could be done by the women,
You men ought to be in the fray,
Not having soft times as we thought you:
But our views are quite different today.

Now it's "Well done, you Linseed Lancers".
You chaps of the R.A.M.C.,
You've worked harder than any department
Of battalions of Infantry.
We've seen you go over the top, chaps,
Where the Allemande guns on you play,
And you've not only done it in darkness,
But you've done it in full light of day.
We've seen you on top of our trenches,

Mud up to your knees and wet through:
You didn't get flustered or windy,
But did your work faithful and true.
We know how your backs have been aching,
But many a life you have saved;
We've seen you around with your stretchers,
As your lives for the wounded you've braved.

So forgive us fer what we have called you;
We're now sorry for what we have said,
For we've seen with our eyes (that's believing),
And the nicknames we called you are dead.
Now we're proud of our brave stretcher-bearers,
You chaps of the R.A.M.C.,
For you've shared all the dangers beside us,
And with kindness you've always been free.
When they ask what we know of you fellows,
We'll tell them in "Blighty" with pride,
That the R.A.M.C. stretcher-bearers
Were the heroes on every side.

By the 'Pack Store Party'.
This poem appeared in the *Journal of the Leeds Territorial Hospitals* in December 1917

MATRONS

Miss Annie Eliza Billington became Matron in 1925, when the hospital was confined to the wooden extension wards.

Miss M Cowie was Matron when she was awarded the Royal Red Cross Medal, First Class (*British Journal of Nursing* 9 August 1919)

Elizabeth Fisher was Principal Matron at some stage. She is mentioned in the Supplement to the Edinburgh Gazette of 20 February 1918 as having moved on from Beckett Park to become Matron at Ingestre Hospital, Ashton-upon-Mersey.

Jessie Ethel Hills was the first Matron at Beckett Park, appointed in good time for the opening of the hospital: she was headhunted by Matron-in-Chief Innes, who must have known her well because she had followed her as Matron at the Halifax Royal Infirmary. A letter in the National Archives at Kew to the Officer in Command at the Second Northern, dated 18 October 1913, recommends her for appointment to the staff. Another letter in the National Archives dated 1931, from the secretary of the TANS (Territorial Army Nursing Service) shows that she remained on the records as Matron until her resignation that year. A replacement was found soon afterwards, so the name of the hospital lived on, until the Second World War. She was, in fact, released from service in March, 1919, so that she could return to her civilian work in Halifax.

During the War, she was sent to France in 1915 to become Matron at the 58th (Scottish) Hospital in St Omer, which was where the General Headquarters of the British Expeditionary Force was situated, along with a transit camp and a large aerodrome. Later, she became Matron of the Portuguese Hospital in France, which served the small numbers of troops from Portugal who were at the front. She was replaced at Beckett Park by Mabel Whiffen.

After the War, now re-established at the Halifax Royal Infirmary, she appeared briefly in a film made in 1925, now in the Yorkshire Film Archive, when Princess Mary and Viscount Lascelles came to open new wards. She posed with the princess on some steps. The Halifax Royal Infirmary closed in 2001, its services transferred to the Calderdale Royal Hospital.

Euphemia Steele Innes, born 1874 in Carnoustie, Scotland, was Matron-in-Chief of the Second Northern General and its attached hospitals throughout the War, with overall responsibility for staffing. She arrived at the Leeds General Infirmary in 1897 to begin her training, and soon held posts as Casualty, Ward and Theatre Sister and Night Superintendent before her appointment to Halifax Royal Infirmary as Assistant Matron in 1907. Two years later she returned to the LGI as Assistant Lady Superintendent, then went back again to Halifax in 1912 as Matron. The following year she became the Lady Superintendant at the LGI, and at the same time was put in charge of the future wartime hospital.

As a member of the Matron's Council of Great Britain and Ireland, she would no doubt have been well aware of national and international dimensions: at the meeting she attended in Wigan in the autumn of 1912, she would have listened to a report by the organisation's Secretary, Miss Mollett, on the International Council Meeting and Congress which was held that year in Cologne, with fifty-seven British delegates. Miss Mollett had admired the "monumental address" of a Dr Hecker, described as a social reformer, although she did add that he had "the cold, calculating precision and overwealth of detail of a German man of science".

She was awarded the Royal Red Cross medal (First Class) in 1916. This was conferred on her by King George V at Buckingham Palace. When she returned to the Infirmary, she was met by a reception party led by Mr Flint, the resident surgical officer, Dr Bibby, the resident medical officer, "and by all the sisters and nurses, who cheered her heartily and escorted her along the main corridors" according the *The British Journal of Nursing* of 29 January, which later mentions "her organizing ability and sympathetic care".

In 1925, she founded The General Infirmary at Leeds Nurses League, which is still thriving today.

Phoebe Elizabeth Smith ARRC was awarded the Royal Red Cross Medal, First Class in 1920.

Mabel Leigh Whiffen was appointed as Matron in May 1915 to replace Jessie Hills.

NURSES AND VADS

Most trained nurses at Beckett Park were members of the QAIMNS (Queen Alexandra's Imperial Military Nursing Service) which was formed in 1902, or of its sister organization the TFNS (Territorial Force Nursing Service) which was formed in 1908. All of them would have qualified after a three-year training course at an approved hospital, and it can be assumed that most of them had plenty of experience. Some of them will have been sent overseas to work in casualty clearing stations or base hospitals near the front. According to Sue Light, on the website of the Western Front Association (http://www.westernfrontassociation.com/), over the course of the Great War, 8,140 women served at some time as mobilized members of the Territorial Force Nursing Service, and of these 2,280 served overseas.

In 1909, the War Office issued 'Scheme for the Organisation of Voluntary Aid in England and Wales' which set up both male and female Voluntary Aid detachments to fill any gaps which might appear in the territorial medical services. In October 1914, responsibility for these passed to a wartime amalgamation of the British Red Cross and the St John's Ambulance Association, which provided preliminary training in first aid and nursing. At the beginning of the war, VADs (as they quickly became known) began to run their own hospitals and auxiliary units (for example at Gledhow Hall in Leeds), and in 1915 they were allowed to augment the staffs of military hospitals at home. This permission was quickly extended to include base hospitals overseas as well, because of increasing demands.

The women who became VADs had a wide range of ages and backgrounds, but they were overwhelmingly from the middle and upper classes – the daughters of professional and business men, army officers and the clergy, who had probably never been in paid employment or worked outside the home. There was a sprinkling of aristocratic women as well. In some hospitals there were tensions with the trained nurses, but there is no evidence this existed at Beckett Park. The most famous memoir of life as a VAD is Testament of Youth by Vera Brittain, published in 1933.

The Royal Red Cross medal, Second Class, was awarded to the following nurses: Sister A B H Bell, Staff Nurse Minnie Byrne, Staff Nurse Winifred L Fry from Auckland, New Zealand, Sister Marie De Mulder, Sister Katherine Irvine, Sister Elizabeth Lindsay.

Nurses and VADs named in the Sprittles scrapbook are: Miss S Aske VAD, Sister V Atha, Sister Batty, Sister A M Bentley, Miss H Crowther VAD, Miss J Denton, Miss G Dove, Sister L W Ford, Miss Nellie Gale VAD, Sister Greer, Miss Habbershaw VAD, Miss Hodgson VAD, Sister Beatrice G Hoyland, Sister V Pratt, Miss Phyllis Russling, and Nurse Mabel Wilson.

VAD Nurse Y Adams from West Otago was 'brought to the notice of the Secretary of State for War (New Zealand), for valuable service rendered in connection with the war'.

Staff Nurse D Alexander is mentioned as being promoted to Sister in 1919 in Sister Pratt's archived records.

Sister E Armstrong from West Otago was 'brought to the notice of the Secretary of State for War (New Zealand), for valuable service rendered in connection with the war'.

VAD Nurse Sophia Violet Barrett, from Ireland, died at sea. Her story is told in 'Torpedoed'.

Nurse J Campbell worked in G1 ward in 1915. Her autograph book, which contains a number of brief messages from some of the patients she looked after, is in the Thackray Medical Museum.

VAD Nurse Florence Lavinia Cunningham is mentioned in the Canadian Great War Project

Staff Nurse N Hanson is mentioned as being promoted to Sister in 1919 in Sister Pratt's archived records.

Sister Louie Johnson was at Beckett Park from May 1915, working in a tetanus ward, before being transferred to East Leeds War Hospital.

Staff Nurse J D Kimpsford served in hospitals in London and at Beckett Park (1915 – 1920). A portrait photograph of Miss Kimpsford and the panorama photograph of the staff of Beckett Park taken October 1917, is held by the IWM's Photograph Archive. This is the same panorama photograph as the one in Annie Storey's souvenirs in Special Collections, Brotherton Library. Her medals and undress ribbons mounted on a brooch bar are also at the IWM. Catalogue number OMD 2776-2777.

Sister A Murgatroyd from West Otago was 'brought to the notice of the Secretary of State for War (New Zealand), for valuable service rendered in connection with the war'.

Staff Nurse E A Noblett wrote a prizewinning paper (October 1915) for the *British Journal of Nursing* in response to the question "What is a 'saline' (saline fluid)? Give its uses, and describe the method of giving a rectal saline." She wrote another prizewinning paper for the same publication (in 1916) in response to "State generally the symptoms of gastric ulcer, and the dangers arising therefrom. How would you feed a patient suffering from this disease?"

VAD Nurse E T Pegge from West Otago was 'brought to the notice of the Secretary of State for War (New Zealand), for valuable service rendered in connection with the war'

Sister Emily Violet Pratt is featured in "Hot-tempered, but dedicated'

Sister Mary Louise Stollard is well-known for a couple of vivid quotations from her articles, which are on various websites. Her writing appeared in magazines and newspapers, including The *Daily Mail,* usually signed 'Sister Mary Stollard'. She was born in Tewkesbury in 1885, and trained at Leeds General Infirmary, being listed as a resident of the nurses' home on the 1911 Census. She worked at Beckett Park as a QAIMNS member.

The most-quoted extracts from her writing are as follows: "They were pathetic, these shell-shocked boys, and a lot of them were very sensitive about the fact that they were incontinent. They'd say 'I'm terribly sorry about it, Sister, it's shaken me all over and I can't control it. Just imagine, to wet the bed at my age!'"

So many of the writings on patients which still exist are from medical men who are necessarily cool and objective. It is good to hear an emotionally engaged voice: "All that winter we took in bronchitis and rheumatism cases. Some of the bronchitis patients were as bad as the men who were gassed, but the rheumatism cases really were the worst. It was pathetic to see these young men absolutely crippled with rheumatism, sometimes doubled up as if they were men of eighty instead of boys in their twenties. We set up a special department to treat them with hot baths and heat treatment, massage and electrical treatment. Most of them got better, but some of them had to be discharged from the army because the rheumatism had taken such a hold. They suffered terrible pain with it. They came out of the wet trenches simply crippled with rheumatism."

(From Chapter 14 *The Roses of No Man's Land* by Lyn Macdonald)

Sister Annie Storey was at the hospital throughout the war. See 'Annie Storey's Souvenirs'

Staff Nurse Rita Trevethen died while on active service in Mesopotamia. A prayer desk with a brass inscription was made in her memory, paid for by staff.

Staff Nurse B M Wilson from West Otago, was 'brought to the notice of the Secretary of State for War (New Zealand), for valuable service rendered in connection with the war'

Staff Nurse M E Wilson is mentioned as being promoted to Sister in 1919 in Sister Pratt's archived records.

Staff Nurse A M Woolley from West Otago was 'brought to the notice of the Secretary of State for War (New Zealand), for valuable service rendered in connection with the war'

Staff Nurse M I Wright is mentioned as being promoted to Sister in 1919 in Sister Pratt's archived records.

RAMC MEN

These are the known RAMC men who were not doctors or surgeons

Private Patrick Hession was born in 1898 in Woodlesford, Leeds, where he lived with five brothers and sisters and his parents, Irish-born William and Yorkshire-born Mary. He became a private in the RAMC and worked at Beckett Park, before he was sent to the front. Aged nineteen, he was killed in action on 5 December 1917, the details and circumstances unknown. He is buried in a military cemetery near Ypres.

Private Henry Kellett is pictured in the Sprittles scrapbook wearing a white coat and standing by a workbench in what appears to be a laboratory. A Bunsen burner and plaster moulds for dentures can be seen, so it is safe to assume that he was a dental technician in the RAMC. He died on 16 March 1917 at the hospital, cause unknown.

Captain Alec Coleman Mackie enlisted in the RAMC as a despatch rider (messenger) in August 1914, and later drove an ambulance based at Beckett Park. In January 1915, he was commissioned into the 17th Battalion of the West Yorkshire Regiment and appointed Machine Gun Officer. He fought in France from May 1916, and later that year broke his nose, which was the reason he was evacuated to Britain, and a place he knew well, Beckett Park. After a brief stay, he was given command of the 253rd Machine Gun Company which moved to Colchester for special training. It was then sent to Murmansk, in June 1918, to fight against the Bolsheviks and to try to keep Russia in the war. His letters home are in the Imperial War Museum, and are described as 'jovial and optimistic in tone' even though he was part of the Somme offensive. (IWM Catalogue Number Documents 22057/ private papers)

Private Thomas Jubb Neilson was not as young as he looked: he was born in Leeds in 1896, the son of Thomas Neilson, an architect, and Alice Jubb. He is on the 1901 Census at the age of five, living with his maternal aunt Emily Jubb at The Villa, Barkston, and on the 1911 Census he is living at 3, Quarry Mount, Hyde Park, Leeds. He married Doris Hudson, who lived in Ash Grove, Headingley, on 22 December, 1927 at Wrangthorn, St Augustine's Church, and is described as an insurance inspector on the certificate, which his father signed as one of the witnesses. In the forties and the sixties he is listed in phone books as living at 20, Broomfield Crescent, Headingley – a long-term resident. He died in December 1983 in Salford, aged 87. He was on the staff at Beckett Park, and a member of the 2nd West Riding Field Ambulance.

Quartermaster Sergeant Alexander Robert Reilly was awarded the Meritorious Service Medal when he left Becket Park in 1919. He was living in Grosvenor Place, Leeds, at the time. George Sprittles pasted an invitation to his retirement party into his scrapbook - 'A Farewell Supper and Smoking Concert' on Thursday 17 July 1919. It must have been a significant event in the sergeant's mess, with a supper at 7pm and a 'smoker' at 8pm. The invitation card was well printed by men in the Curative Workshops. Reilly was one of the older men on the staff, born at Aldershot in 1862, his father a Scot in the army there. He was brought up in Gomersal and later moved to Delph Lane, Leeds.

Sergeant Arthur Sheard was a member of the RAMC serving at Beckett Park. He appears in several photos in the Sprittles scrapbook. He was born 1890 in Leeds, the son of Samuel and Ann Sheard, his father a tool fitter. The 1901 census has the eleven year-old Arthur living with his parents, four sisters and three brothers, the oldest aged twenty-four, the youngest aged one. In 1911 he is down in the census as being a compositor in the printing industry. He was discharged from the Army in March, 1918, his papers giving his address as 38, Rosebank Road, Belle Vue Road, Leeds and his military character as 'very good', but tuberculosis had been discovered in his body, possibly picked up from a patient. He was recommended for sanatorium treatment, because he was 'easily tired', but no evidence has been found that he got this. There was a diminution in the number of deaths from tuberculosis in 1919 (*British Medical Journal* 5 February 1921), but it was still a major worry, and it is remarkable that the fall in the mortality rate took place, considering that the flu epidemic continued into the early part of that year. Arthur died 16 April 1919 aged twenty-nine, and was buried with honours in Lawnswood Cemetery.

Private James Dudley Sinnett RAMC came from Haverfordwest in Wales. He was working as a nurse in Marylebone, London prior to the war, and enlisted there on 27 January 1916 into the Royal Army Medical Corps. He worked at Beckett Park before being posted to the 35th Company, RAMC. He died of pneumonia at Queen Alexandra's Military Hospital, Millbank on 13 January 1918, aged 27. He was buried at St. Martin Cemetery, Haverfordwest, and his name is on the brass war memorial inside St Thomas a Beckett's church. (Information from West Wales War Memorial Project)

Sergeant George Sprittles is in 'Thanks, George'.

HELP! HELP, IT'S COLD!

Nurses of course, had to be modest and angelic all the time. Imagine the gasps or sniggers from readers of *The British Journal of Nursing* in January 1916 when they read this article. The royal 'we' used by the writer may indicate that she was a matron.

"Why is it that when women leave this country they so often think it unnecessary to observe the proprieties, and sometimes we must add the decencies of civilized life? The fact is painfully brought home to us by a picture which has been published in more than one of the illustrated papers, representing a doctor in a bath lightly clad in a shirt, while round him stand a group of shameless women in pyjamas, several with their hair down their backs, guffawing and drenching their victim with water. Over the picture are the words, "Help! Help, it's cold! The doctor is given a shower bath," and below the note, "Outnumbered by eight to one the doctor had no chance to escape, and had, in popular parlance, to 'go through with it.' The nurses were without mercy or compassion, and poured cold water over him, in addition to scrubbing him with the hardest brushes. The photograph was taken in Serbia."

Our attention has been drawn to this disgraceful picture by several correspondents, one of whom writes: "If this photograph is genuine it is surely imperative that a public inquiry should be made by an authority in the nursing world, as to the training school responsible for such a doctor and such nurses, and Matron-in-Charge.

These nurses do not appear to have even the excuse of youth, though few young girls in the privacy of their home would indulge in such horse play or exhibit themselves in such attire, and is it possible that any qualified man would permit such behaviour on the part of his nurses?

"No wonder the French express astonishment at the un-nurselike appearance of some of our women – high-heeled shoes, white silk stockings, perfumes etc – and that our wounded are not always satisfied with the class of nurse chosen to tend them? It is a scandal that such creatures should be let loose on helpless sick and wounded and allowed to disgrace our country abroad."

It would be interesting to know who selected and sent these women, trained or untrained, to Serbia. The pernicious interference in of unprofessional people with nursing affairs since the war began has led to more scandal than it was possible to imagine."

ARMY MEDICINE

Medical advances and innovations have often resulted from extreme wartime conditions. At the outbreak of the English Civil War (1642–1651) MPs passed a bill which recognized for the first time that Parliament had a duty of care towards soldiers killed or wounded in its service, and towards widows and orphans. The first hospital for military patients was established at this time. The first mobile field hospitals can be dated to 1692, on the battlefields of the Nine Years War in Ireland and Flanders.

In 1752, the Scottish doctor John Pringle published the first major scientific account outlining strategies to prevent and control disease: *Observations on the Diseases of the Army*. He recognized that hospitals were among the main causes of sickness and death. In 1789, the anatomist John Hunter, often mentioned by Sir Berkeley Moynihan as one of his greatest predecessors, was responsible for the creation of the Standing Army's first permanent hospital in Chelsea.

During the wars with Napoleon, disease, usually the result of poor hygiene, was the biggest killer. Surgeons treated a large proportion of wounds by amputation, using the same blades and saws repeatedly and washing their hands in dirty water, if at all. Pain was considered to be an unavoidable part of an operation, but gin or brandy might have been available for some of the luckier wounded. Not much had changed by the time of the Crimean War in 1853, when the Army's medical services were appallingly inefficient, with 20,000 British soldiers dying, of whom only 1600 were killed in battle. Anaesthetics were available in the form of chloroform. The invention of the telegraph and the presence of a correspondent from *The Times* of London - William Howard Russell – resulted in public outrage. Florence Nightingale and her team of volunteer nurses improved conditions greatly, mainly by cleaning up the hospital in Scutari, Turkey, and Jamaican herbalist and nurse Mary Seacole travelled at her own expense to set up the 'British Hotel' for wounded officers just behind the front line.

The Army Nursing Service was set up in 1881, and its members soon saw action in the Boer Wars in South Africa (1880–81 and 1899–1902), the Egyptian Campaign (1882) and the Sudan War (1883 - 85). There was no plan to increase its numbers in the event of a major conflagration. Typhoid, which had ravaged armies previously, was checked in 1897 by the development of a vaccine at the Army Medical School, and at the beginning of the First World War, most British troops had been vaccinated. In 1898, X-Ray machines were used for the first time, which meant that items like bullets and shrapnel could be located and removed before they led to infection. In the same year, all officers and men involved in the medical services were incorporated into the newly-created Royal Army Medical Corps. Medical officers were placed on an equal footing with combatant and other non-combatant branches of the Army.

Queen Alexandra's Imperial Military Medical Service Reserve (QAIMNS) was formed in 1902 in response to deficiencies which had come to light in the Boer Wars.

King Edward VII and Queen Alexandra opened the Royal Army Medical College at Millbank, London in 1907. The following year saw the creation of new voluntary reserve forces, to be mobilized when necessary: there was increasing national agitation about a possible major conflict with the German Empire. The Territorial Force Nursing Service was created. All of the staff nurses at Beckett Park had T.F.N.S. after their names, and most had Q.A.I.M.N.S. there as well. Most of the doctors and surgeons at Beckett Park had joined the territorial reserve years before the start of the war.

The First World War was the first one in which mortality from battle injuries was greater than deaths from diseases, which was due to improved sanitation, preventative medicine and more efficient casualty evacuation procedures – ambulances with petrol engines and dedicated trains replaced horse-drawn vehicles – but the weaponry had vastly increased killing power. The first encounters with the German Army by the more professional but considerably smaller British Expeditionary Force at Mons and the battles which followed soon afterwards caused a series of shocks and surprises. Many of the experienced medics and nurses knew about fighting on the dry South African veldt, where wounds were comparatively clean and combatants did not often fight from trenches, but not much about mechanized warfare, which brought horrific new injuries, limbs smashed by shells fired from the efficient new artillery and wounds which became infected with tetanus or gas gangrene at great speed because of wet farmland conditions.

Head wounds, and injuries to eyes, face and jaws were particularly common because of the nature of trench warfare, which made the upper parts of bodies vulnerable. Trench periscopes lessened the risks to some extent, but steel helmets were not issued to the British until the end of 1915. The Germans continued to wear the boiled leather Pickelhaube (spiked helmet) well into 1916. Treatment of facial injuries, one of the specialities at Beckett Park, led to advances in maxillofacial surgery and plastic surgery

At the Second battle of Ypres in 1915, poison gas in the form of chlorine was used for the first time by the Germans. Most of the thousands of victims had no protection. Not much could be done at aid posts and casualty clearing stations. Early responses included the use of cotton pads dipped into a solution of bicarbonate of soda, but by the end of the war effective gas masks were in use. Respiratory problems caused by gas inhalation were amongst those treated at Beckett Park.

In 1915, Sir Robert Jones, often described as the father of modern British orthopaedics, introduced the Thomas splint, which had been devised by his uncle Hugh Owen Thomas. This was for fractures of the femur (thigh bone) and it dramatically reduced the mortality rate. In 1918, American surgeons improved on the design, which was used long after the end of the war.

The Queen's Hospital, Sidcup, opened in June 1917. This specialized in the treatment of severe facial injuries. Sir Harold Gillies was the force behind the hospital. He had developed new techniques. He used tubular 'pedicles' (flaps of skin) to retain blood flow to the flesh while it is grafted from the undamaged area on to the injured area. Gillies and his colleagues carried out more than 11,000 operations on 5,000 men at the Queen's Hospital. The first plastic surgery patient, naval officer Walter Yeo, severely wounded in the face whilst manning the guns on HMS Warspite during the Battle of Jutland in 1916, was given new eyelids and a skin 'mask' which was grafted across his face and eyes.

The National Blood Transfusion Service has its origins in the first successful attempts to store human blood on the Western Front thanks to earlier advances with anti-coagulants and blood-typing. The Army set up the first blood depot in the world, which stored O type blood, suitable for all recipients.

Eighty thousand cases of 'shell shock' had been recorded by the end of the war, but there was not much by way of sympathy for them from the Army. Early treatments ranged from solitary confinement and disciplinary action to 'physical re-education' and electric shock treatment. Few doctors, civilian or military, had much idea of what they could or should do. Read Pat Barker's *Regeneration* (1991) to find out about Dr W H R Rivers, an army psychiatrist who worked at Craiglockhart War Hospital, and his relationship with the poet Siegfried Sassoon, who made a public declaration against the continuation of the war and who had been labeled as shell shocked.

In 1921, dentists in the RAMC were split off to form the Army Dental Corps, but it did not get the "Royal" prefix until after the Second World War.

• HOSPITAL BLUES •

As at other hospitals and convalescent establishments, wounded soldiers at Beckett Park were issued with a special uniform – a single-breasted flannelette jacket with a white lining, worn open at the neck, blue trousers, a white shirt and a red tie. The khaki service cap with its regimental badge was to be worn as well. There were no pockets, for some reason.

It was not particularly popular, mainly because it was sometimes too large and often fitted badly: when it was washed, the lining tended to shrink at a different rate to the rest of the uniform, which was made of a different material. It was sometimes known as the 'blue invalid uniform'.

I wish those people who write so glibly about this being a holy war and the orators who talk so much about going on, no matter how long the war lasts and what it may mean, could see a case of mustard gas - the poor things burnt and blistered all over with great mustard coloured suppurating blisters, with blind eyes, all sticky and stuck together, and always fighting for breath, with voices a mere whisper, saying their throats are closing and they know they will choke. (From *Testament of Youth* by Vera Brittain)

THE EVACUATION ROUTE

These are the levels in a complex casualty evacuation system which a man wounded on the Western Front would probably have gone through in his rearward movement to Beckett Park. The speed of progression from one level to the next could be quick, or he could spend days, or even weeks at one of the levels, for example at a base hospital. It all depended on his condition. Sometimes levels could be missed out.

Regimental Aid Post

At full strength, up to thirty orderlies and stretcher bearers under the RMO (Regimental Medical Officer) would staff one of these, which would be in, or very close to, the front line, possibly in a dugout, a communication trench or a deep shell hole. It could provide emergency treatment, often rudimentary.

Advanced Dressing Station

This would be immediately behind the front line, usually in a protected location like an underground dug-out or bunker. Stretcher cases and walking wounded would be given immediate care while they waited to be taken on further. RAMC men from the Field Ambulance were in charge

Field Ambulance

A mobile unit with motorized or horse-drawn ambulances. These often had a circular route to take the wounded to the CCS. The Field Ambulance was the most forward of the RAMC units and the first line of documentation. When the Division was not in action on the line, it could be allocated a special task such as a scabies centre or a bath unit.

Casualty Clearing Station

This was very large, and more often than not under canvas, though huts were erected if possible. It was located a few miles behind the lines, preferably near a railway line. It could typically accommodate a thousand cases, but might be overwhelmed by the wounded resulting from a major battle. Most amputations would be performed here. In 'normal' circumstances, it would be staffed by seven medical officers, one quartermaster and seventy-seven other ranks. There would also be a dentist, a pathologist, seven QAIMNS nurses and other non-medical personnel attached. X-Ray was normally available. Serious cases would stay until they were fit for travel, slight ones would be patched up and sent back to their units and most would be sent on as soon as possible. 'Blighty cases' might be taken directly to a port of embarkation, but the next stop was often a base hospital. Today, a large military cemetery often marks the place where a CCS was.

Base Hospital

Most casualties would arrive here in an ambulance train, which might be of British or French origin, fitted out with accommodation for stretcher cases and some equipment. The journey could take a long time: troop trains and supply trains had priority. It might be called a Stationary or a General Hospital, and would be near an army base, for example at Etaples, Boulogne, Le Havre, Rouen or Le Touquet. It could be situated in an existing hospital or in a requisitioned hotel or even casino. Pathological research took place at some of them. As always, the RAMC would organize everything, but each hospital had three chaplains. Towards the end of the war, a base hospital could have up to two and a half thousand beds.

Hospital Ship

A hospital ship was a cargo or passenger vessel which had been requisitioned for the duration of the war and adapted for purpose. Western Front casualties would cross the Channel in one, perhaps from Le Havre to Southampton. There was some risk that the ship might be torpedoed by a U-boat or hit a mine.

Ambulance Train

At the port of arrival, casualties would be put on a train which might take them directly to Leeds, or perhaps they might go to another war hospital first. They would be met at the Midland Station, Leeds, by ambulances, often driven by volunteers and transported to Beckett Park, or to East Leeds War Hospital.

WARTIME DISEASES AND INFECTIONS

Cerebrospinal fever, meningococcal meningitis, had a heavy mortality rate. An acute inflammation of the meninges of the brain and spinal cord, it was accompanied by fever and sometimes red spots on the skin. There was considerable anxiety about this disease, not only because it was present amongst troops on the Western Front, but because it had become common amongst the civil and the military population at home. The chief epidemic strains were identified during the First World War and a serum 'of curative potency' (*British Medicine in the War* BMA 1917) was developed in 1915. Isolation of all carriers was impractical, so this was done only with those infected with epidemic strains. In some hospitals, chronic carriers were made to breathe for a short time the air of a room saturated with a fine spray of chloramine-T, a mild disinfectant. The principal pathologist, Major Wilfrid Vining, dealt with cases at Beckett Park, usually sending them on (with Tetanus cases) to Killingbeck Hospital.

Diphtheria is a bacterial illness affecting the tonsils, pharynx and nose which has been just about eradicated in Britain by inoculation programmes. Its symptoms are often a greatly swollen neck or a kind of grey membrane appearing at the back of the throat, and it was often fatal – quickly. Severe cases today are put into intensive care.

Dysentery, also known as the bloody flux, is an inflammatory disorder of the intestines, particularly the colon, which causes severe diarrhoea containing blood and mucus as well as faecal matter. It has a variety of causes, including viral or bacterial infections and parasitic infestations. It can lead to abdominal pain, fever and delirium. The only preventative measures which worked involved paying special attention to hygiene, which was less practicable in the Mediterranean war zone: wounded men arriving from Gallipoli often suffered from dysentery, of both the bacterial and the amoebic sorts.

Enteric fever (typhoid and paratyphoid fever) was "the great medical scourge of all former wars" but "has been reduced in this, the greatest of all wars, to insignificant proportions" wrote Dr F W Andrewes in *British Medicine in the War* (BMA 1917). It is still a common bacterial disease all over the world, transmitted by the ingestion of food or water contaminated with the faeces of an infected person, which contain the relevant bacterium. Inoculation treatment for the Army had been pioneered in the Boer War, and was taken up again in the First World War. Even so, large numbers of enteric fever cases were noted on the hospital ships which took men off the Gallipoli peninsula.

Gas Gangrene, or Myonecrosis, is the deadliest form of gangrene, and is rarely encountered today. It is caused by bacteria which live in the soil. It was near impossible to give adequate fast and sterile treatment for battle wounds, especially in the first years of the war before the use of the Carrel-Dakin apparatus (when it was available) which provided constant irrigation of wounds with a specially devised antiseptic fluid. Consequently, large numbers of soldiers died after myonecrosis (muscle tissue death) set in along with sepsis and gas production under the skin which caused large black blisters. This could happen after a relatively small wound, for example one caused by a piece of shrapnel which had entered the body taking with it tiny fragments of dirty uniform, or after a large one. Fast amputations of infected limbs saved lives.

Influenza, or Spanish Flu, killed more people than the First World War between 1918 and 1919, somewhere between twenty and forty million people worldwide. More people died in one year than in four years of bubonic plague between 1347 and 1351. It was a particularly virulent strain of influenza, with a mortality rate of 2.5 percent as compared to the usual rate of 0.1 percent. The death rate for those aged between fifteen and thirty-five was many times higher than in previous years: the virus had evolved to affect younger people in particular. Patients with what seemed at first to be an ordinary type of influenza would suddenly develop an extremely vicious form of pneumonia which would make them struggle desperately for breath until they suffocated quickly, their lungs clogged up with a kind of jelly. There is not much to read about the pandemic (a word frowned upon by the General Medical Council at the time) and newspapers buried stories about it at the bottoms of pages, reluctant to write about, or disbelieving the extent, of this new killer after so much reporting of war fatalities. Doctors could not do much, and there was no antidote with the alleged potency of Tamiflu. Priority was given to the wounded by the medical services. In the streets, it was common to see people wearing masks made of butter muslin, Oxo ran an expensive advertising campaign which claimed that drinking its meaty product would 'fortify the system', coffins were suddenly in short supply and many children were kept away from school by worried parents. In the absence of adequate records, it is impossible to say what the effect of influenza was at Beckett Park, but it must have exercised many minds there.

Tetanus, also known as Lockjaw, is usually due to contaminated wounds. It causes muscle spasms which affect the jaws, extremities, back, abdomen and diaphragm. Breathing becomes difficult, and a quarter of those affected (today) die. It was responsible for many deaths in the manured farmlands of France and Flanders, because the bacterium which causes the disease only survives in anaerobic conditions deep in the soil – which was dug into for trenches. In the first year of the war, tetanus cases could fill a whole ward, but after the introduction of an effective serum, it became rarer.

Trench fever is a bacterial infection transmitted by body lice. It infected all of the armies on both sides of the conflict, with nearly a third of British troops picking it up at some time or another: lice were almost impossible to avoid, living in the seams of unwashed clothing. It can lead to heart failure, but deaths were relatively rare. Literary victims include J R R Tolkien, who came down with the disease in October 1916 and who was sent to recuperate in a hospital in England when he was a second lieutenant. In 1920, the great man was appointed as a reader in the English department at the University of Leeds, living in Headingley within very easy walking distance of Beckett Park. Did he ever visit, I wonder?

Trench foot is an infection of the feet caused by wet, cold and dirty conditions, like waterlogged trenches. Men were unable to take off their wet socks and boots, or not motivated to do so when they were exhausted or when it was freezing cold. The skin on numb feet turns red or blue, and gangrene can result if nothing is done, which is followed by amputation. In 1915, orders were given that each soldier in the trenches should carry three pairs of socks, to change them twice a day, dry the feet thoroughly and to rub whale oil into them. Men were paired off, with one responsible for the other's feet. Trench foot can develop quickly: a few cases have been recorded at the Glastonbury Festival.

Trench mouth (gingivitis) is a severe gum infection caused by bacteria accumulating in the mouth. Gums bleed and ulcers develop. It is caused by poor dental hygiene. The teeth of many new recruits were recorded as being in poor condition during the war, and at first they were often rejected if they were too bad.

Trench nephritis (inflammation of the kidneys) had causes which were unknown during the war, in spite of the extensive international research into them. It first became serious in the spring of 1915: affected soldiers were breathless, with swollen faces or legs, headaches and sore throats. It was a serious problem for the Allies, with thousands hospitalized and hundreds of deaths.

Tuberculosis was a major cause of infectious disease death in soldiers. Extremely drug resistant tuberculosis now exists which in some patients is clinically the same as the tuberculosis of the First World War, in the pre-antibiotic period. By the time of the war, the old name of consumption had long been dropped for this ancient disease, but there were no effective modern treatments, and it was as fatal as it had been for John Keats nearly a century previously. Efforts were made to exclude men from military service who were known to have TB, and there is evidence in medical records of patients at Beckett Park who were routinely checked for it.

Venereal diseases (Sexually Transmitted Diseases) were a major problem nationally, but were not much written about, except perhaps in a coy way, by journalists. Many thousands of soldiers of all countries became infected. In New Zealand, for example, General George Richardson told the defence minister that about 7,600 New Zealand soldiers were being infected annually. Soldiers were warned of the risks, and 'dangle parades' were sometimes held to check the genitals for symptoms, but brothels, large and small, were everywhere in the war zone. After the war, there was a global pandemic of syphilis and gonorrhoea following the return home of the troops. 'Loose women' were blamed, of course, and there were some syphilis - prevention films made by the YMCA, but condoms were not promoted by Britain or the United States (unlike other countries) in case they encouraged immorality. Treatment for syphilis would have been Salvarsan (Arsphenamine) if it was available, which had been discovered in 1906 in the laboratory of the German scientist Paul Ehrlich. Gonorrhoea was mainly treated by urethral washouts using medicated fluids, which must have been unpopular. There were probably 'VD' cases at Beckett Park, but no records.

> Moral attitudes shifted: when it became clear that the exodus of men to the front had left thousands of unmarried mothers pregnant, their children were declared patriotic 'war babies' and money raised to support them. Other forms of support made breakthroughs too: the bra began to oust the old-fashioned camisole. One diplomatist said later that when he had left England in 1911 'contraceptives were hard to buy outside London or other large cities. By 1919 every village chemist was selling them." (From *The Making of Modern Britain* by Andrew Marr)

SHELL SHOCK

Causations

While physical and emotional responses to the dangers and discomforts of trench warfare, particularly the less dramatic ones, were extremely common, enough behaviours, inexplicable by any obvious physical cause, were displayed by British servicemen to cause considerable concern among both military and medical authorities. These concerns peaked in 1916 when the number of casualties suffering from symptoms with no apparent direct causation by either arms or disease, reached epidemic levels. In the last six months of the year some 16,000 men were diagnosed as 'shell shock sick'.

Prior to this, the condition of 'shell shock' had been known about within the British military but was deemed a marginal medical problem. The term itself had been coined by the Cambridge psychologist Dr Charles Myers, who had been recruited to the Army Medical Service in 1914. In a 1915 article for *The Lancet,* Myers discussed three cases of men whose symptoms had appeared following close proximity to shell explosions. The argument supported the 'commotional' theory of causation, put forward by Myers's neurologist colleague Gordon Holmes, which held that the percussive force of an explosion cause microscopic damage to the brain and nervous system. By 1916, however, Myers had disavowed his own term in favour of ideas which emphasised the psychological nature of the disorder as a psychic response to danger, discomfort and, above all, fear. He began advocating strongly for the rapid treatment of those suffering from the symptoms, emphasising that these men were not mad or cowards, but rather temporarily unnerved and capable of recovery through a period of rest and psychological treatment.

By this time the military authorities were both increasingly concerned about the implications for wastage of manpower that an epidemic of incurable nervous responses threatened, and convinced that the weakness it appeared to expose was contagious, with one shell-shocked soldier within a unit causing others to suffer, or pretend to suffer, from the condition as well. In response, they forbad the use of the term 'shell shock' as a diagnosis in favour of the less vibrant phrase, 'Not Yet Diagnosed (Nervous)'. In fact, individual doctors, both on the front line and in Base and Home hospitals, continued to use a number of terms to cover the wide variety of nervous symptoms that men continued to present with, including hysteria, most often used to refer to functional responses, neurasthenia, most often used with reference to emotional responses and general terms such as 'war neurosis'. In the meantime the term 'shell shock' had entered wider public consciousness, appearing in articles in *The Times,* among others, where it was used as a useful and seemingly comprehensible label for an otherwise frightening and inexplicable manifestation of the effects of war on the human mind.

Treatments

The range of treatments for the nervous disorders of war were as variable as the range of terms used to describe it. While initially the majority of sufferers had been sent back to hospitals in

Britain, where separation from the support of both civilian family and military unit meant their condition often worsened and became entrenched, the flood of casualties in 1916 encouraged the military authorities to give Myers the opportunity to develop specialist treatment units near the front line. Here men were allowed to rest and were treated with a very basic form of psychological therapy based heavily on suggestion. This development coincided with an increased specialisation across the Army Medical Service (AMS), which included the development of specialist units for orthopaedics and abdominal surgery, among others. By 1917 this was taken a step further, with Regimental Medical Officers (RMOs) ordered to keep a man with his unit, rather than sending him down the line to a Casualty Clearing Station (CCS) and specialist unit, if they believed him to be only temporarily shaken. Treatment within the unit varied depending on the RMO involved, with some prescribing rest, sleep and paternalistic chats, while others used the invocation of peer pressure and the fear of losing face in front of comrades to force men back into appropriately soldierly behaviour.

For men who were evacuated to Base or to Britain, the range of treatments was even more broad. At one extreme was the Queen's Square method, named after the hospital where it was employed by Lewis Yealland, who used the application of electric shocks both to stimulate paralysed muscles and to reinforce the medical and military authority of the doctor who was ordering his patient back to health. A superficially gentler method was the variation on Freud's talking cure employed by W.H.R. Rivers at Craiglockhart War Hospital in Scotland, most famously on the poet Siegfried Sassoon, although the levels of potentially coercive suggestion employed even in this method were high. Certainly Sassoon reflected a sense of moral pressure to conform and support his military comrades in his account of his treatment in his fictionalised memoir, *Sherston's Progress*. Other treatments included straightforward hypnotic suggestion, 'ergotherapy', a form of work therapy advocated by the poet Wilfred Owen's doctor, A.J. Brock, and the Weir-Mitchell treatment, which involved bed rest and complete isolation for the patient.

Long-term effects

The results of such treatments were mixed. Sassoon and Owen were among those who returned to the armed forces, Owen to be killed in the last week of the war. Many, however, did not and some, like the poet Ivor Gurney, were to suffer from the long-term effects of war neuroses for the rest of their lives. Nor was it only those who were diagnosed during the conflict who suffered from the after-effects of psychological damage. By 1929 71,466 awards for nervous diseases had been made by the Ministry of Pensions, of which 6,095 were first awards, that is were awards officially recognising a diagnosis for the first time between 1920 and 1929. The psychological damage that war caused continued to be evident throughout British society, particularly for individuals. For sufferers and their families, post-war life with long-term psychological disability was often extremely problematic. Men found it difficult to get and retain work, particularly in the fragile post-war economy. With unemployment levels peaking at 22% in 1932, work was hard to come by for the healthy and able-bodied, let alone those in receipt of a pension for a disability unconnected to a physical wound. Men in receipt of a pension, and therefore a diagnosis, often suffered from prevalent stigmas that associated any form of psychological disorder with madness. These difficulties with employment in turn posed a direct challenge to men's subjective civilian identities as independent wage earners and self-sufficient heads of household, challenges which, for some, exacerbated their psychological disability. Other challenges that men faced included the fact that, when undergoing any treatment provided by the Ministry of Pensions, they might find themselves separated from their families in distant hospitals, and sometimes forbidden from seeing them altogether. Many marriages broke down. In other families wives and elderly parents found themselves assuming emotional and financial responsibility for the care of men who were unable to care for themselves.

There were also profound cultural impacts arising from the long-term effects of psychological disability. Many individuals from the interwar period had vividly recalled encounters with shell-shocked men, including the author Roald Dahl, who wrote of one of his schoolmasters who

was never still. His orange head twitched and jerked perpetually from side to side
in the most alarming fashion, and each twitch was accompanied by a little grunt that came
out of the nostrils ... Rumour had it that the constant twitching and jerking and
snorting was caused by something called shell-shock, but we were not quite sure what that was.
We took it to mean that an explosive object had gone off very close to him with such
an enormous bang that it had made him jump high in the air and he hadn't
stopped jumping since.

By 1940, Robert Graves and Alan Hodge could assert that 'everyone who had been under two or three rolling barrages, was an invalid.' The term 'shell shock' remained part of the cultural language in Britain throughout the 20th century and, with the revival of interest in the First World War, following the fiftieth anniversary of the war years, it came to represent the symbolic wound of the war, emblematic of the suffering of all soldiers who had fought. Literary depictions, such as Pat Barker's *Regeneration* trilogy, and political campaigns, such as the Shot at Dawn campaign for the pardoning of 306 soldiers shot for cowardice, on the grounds that they all suffered from shell shock, whether diagnosed or not, have cemented the condition's status in British culture as universal and emblematic.

By **Dr Jessica Meyer,** University of Leeds

1. Ben Shephard, A War of Nerves: Soldiers and Psychiatrists 1914-1994, London 2002.

2. Siegfried Sassoon, Sherston's Progress, London 1937.

3. Roald Dahl, Boy, London 1984, 108-118.

4. Robert Graves and Alan Hodge, The Long Week-end: A Social History of Great Britain 1918-1939, New York 1940, 16.

I sat up straight and as I did so something inside my head moved like the weights on a doll's eyes and it hit me inside in back of my eyeballs. My legs felt warm and wet and my shoes were wet and warm inside. I knew that I was hit and leaned over and put my hand on my knee. My knee wasn't there. (From *A Farewell to Arms* by Ernest Hemingway)

AMERICAN ASSISTANCE

American surgeons were working at the hospital from 1917. In a fuzzy commemorative photo taken on the main steps in October of that year, the caps worn by some of the men in uniform standing behind Dr Walter Page, the American Ambassador, show that they are from across the Atlantic. Dr Page's visit to officially open new extensions came in the same year that the United States entered the war, in spite of President Woodrow Wilson's efforts to keep his country out of it. A small but significant number of American citizens had been unofficially involved since the beginning, either fighting (through joining up in Canada, for example) or on the medical side. The American Field Service (AFS) was one of several volunteer ambulance services in France during the First World War, which used many drivers with literary backgrounds, amongst them E E Cummings, John Dos Passos and Ernest Hemingway. The American Hospital of Paris, based in the Lycée Pasteur, treated many hundreds from amongst the Allied wounded.

Beckett Park, concentrating mainly on orthopaedic care in the last two years of the war, needed all the extra help it could get. Over half of the serious battle casualties brought back across the Channel in the hospital ships were suffering from what is known in medical terms as chronic conditions of the extremities – that is bones, joints, muscles and nerves. In April, 1917, it was impossible to supply surgical centres with adequate numbers of British surgeons with orthopaedic training, because of the demands of the front. Major General Robert Jones RAMC, one of the foremost orthopaedic surgeons of his day, asked for specialist Americans to be sent over. He wrote: "In 1916 we were ordered to start an orthopedic hospital for military cases in Liverpool, but at that time so short of hospitals were we all over the country that only 250 beds could be afforded to the so-called chronic or orthopaedic cases. At that time it was not fully realized that an ideal orthopedic hospital was primarily intended to prevent the occurrence of disability and deformity, which in so large a proportion of cases were the results of hurried evacuation and inefficient treatment.

The wards were immediately filled with a ghastly array of derelicts. In spite of the fact that we were seriously handicapped for want of staff, the experiment proved so successful that I was practically given a free hand to increase our beds in Liverpool and start similar establishments in other centers. In a few months we had increased our bed accommodation from 250 to nearly 20,000. By degrees the orthopedic hospital was found in London, Leeds, Edinburgh, Aberdeen, Glasgow, Newcastle, Manchester, Bristol, Newport, Cardiff, Dublin, Belfast, and other towns. Instead of dealing merely with cases which resulted from want of continuity in treatment, and which were hopelessly crippled, we received many directly from abroad. This was the opportunity which was needed in order to stem the tide of deformity."

The first group sent over by the United States government consisted of twenty selected men. On their arrival in England they were shown the work being done in the British war hospitals. A few weeks were spent in learning the types of disabilities that were met as the sequel of war wounds and the methods of treatment that had proven efficacious. Then one or two senior medical officers and several junior officers were assigned to the various hospitals in Great Britain, the principal centres being Shepherd's Bush, Oxford, Manchester, Leeds, Edinburgh, Glasgow, Aberdeen, and Cardiff.

The Americans were at once put in charge of wards or services and were made responsible in general to the British surgeons. More intensive study of the cases became possible, along with closer supervision of the treatment. It also made possible better coordination of the various measures used in restoration of function. One man made or helped make the diagnosis, performed or assisted at the operation if one were required, and had charge of the subsequent treatment, which usually consisted of massage, hydrotherapy, electrotherapy, exercises, and work in some 'curative vocation'. The vocations at Beckett Park included basket work, wood turning, jig-saw work, cabinet making, and embroidery. Their contribution was not particularly conspicuous, but it was real and considerable: they added to existing knowledge on overcoming infection and on methods of immobilization, and worked out a system of splinting which built on British innovations (for example the Thomas splint pioneered by Sir Robert Jones) and which simplified the treatment of fractures and joint injuries for years after the war.

In *An Orthopedic Surgeon's Story of the Great War,* by the Nebraska surgeon H. Winnett Orr, MD, the author makes it clear that by the summer of 1916 both the American Orthopedic Association and the American Medical Association were expecting American participation in the war, and formed preparedness committees. The British Commission which came over to the States in 1917 was made very welcome, and the request it brought with it from Sir Robert was dealt with immediately. Orr describes how nerves were on edge as the ship he was on, with its seasick medical passengers, approached the British Isles, because of the fear of German submarines. In Liverpool, Sir Robert himself was there to welcome the surgeons and deliver an up-to-date briefing, and they were entertained at a reception attended by Dr Page and Lady Astor. Orr was impressed in London at the Shepherd's Bush Military Orthopaedic Hospital which was responsible for "some of the best reconstructive surgery in Britain" and which was staffed by "such well-known surgeons as Elmslie, Dunn , Aitken and Bristow".

The visitors had time to see some of the famous sights of the capital, which included Windsor Castle and "the London Tower", and then moved on to look at the rehabilitation work at Roehampton. He was impressed: "The British were facing an immense problem in the care of their men with amputations. Most of them were at home waiting for care. However, at Roehampton, stumps were being improved surgically, deformities were being corrected, temporary and artificial limbs were being put on, and best of all, the vocational schools were really working." The surgeons were then separated into contingents to be sent around the country. According to Orr, the ones sent to Beckett Park, described as the 'British Orthopedic Center, Leeds' were **Major Roades Fayerweather** from Baltimore and **Lieutenant L E Spencer** from New Orleans, but there are also records of **Captain Edward Jelks** from Jacksonville and **Lieutenant Robert Nichol MacGuffie,** originally from Scotland but a native of New York City. MacGuffie was at Beckett Park for just a short while before being sent to work at the front as a regimental medical officer. He was seriously wounded a week or so before the Armistice, on 1 November 1918, when he was wounded at Valenciennes by a shell in both thighs. After two operations in France he was sent to the Third London General Hospital in London, where he remained for seven months. He was then transferred to American Base Hospital, No. 40, at Knotty Ash, Liverpool. He was decorated with the British Military Cross by King George V at Buckingham Palace, in March, 1919, and cited by Sir Douglas Haig for devotion to duty at Mareschs during the Battle of the Salle River, in October, 1918.

All of the surgeons were, of course, white and male. The involvement of new and distinctly different nurses and doctors was a lively topic of conversation in wartime hospitals. The always staunchly patriotic *British Nursing Journal* of 6 July 1918 carried the following under the heading 'Free Coloured Women Helping to Free the World':

'…..Cincinatti… the Mecca of no end of fugitive slaves. Here lived the abolitionists Coffin and Beecher, and here Harriet Beecher Stowe penned her *Uncle Tom's Cabin.* In fact, here, if anywhere, the big fight for the liberty of the black man may be said to have concentrated. In and about Cincinnati still you may find any number of men, or women, who received freedom from the Emancipator President… Now free themselves, at the call to help other lands — in fact, to save all the world from autocracy — these coloured women are not to be behindhand in the good work. Affiliated with the Red Cross — in fact, now one of its definite units — they have formed a Soldiers' Comfort Club, originally for providing various creature comforts for the coloured soldiers, but now given over to all the regular Red Cross activities.

On Liberty Day, the first anniversary of America's taking definite share in the stupendous conflict, Cincinnati marked the opening of the big drive for the Third American Liberty Loan with one of the largest parades in her history. Among others, the Red Cross workers turned out, marching in their attractive white habits and veils, the endless cohorts having their snowy whiteness punctuated by the red caps of supervisors here and there. Boundless applause greeted all these workers along the line of march; but no one unit received more acclaim than the one hundred and fifty negro women of the Soldiers' Comfort Club — the dusky faces of these faithful knitters and sewers and the makers of dressings and comforts for the sick all the more picturesque, in contrast with their white attire. As black troops are available from America to take part in the war in Europe, the President of the National Association of Coloured Graduate Nurses offers 2 ,000 black nurses, ready-trained for service at military hospitals in Europe and America…'

A HIGHLY CONTENTIOUS MATTER

The question of the reallocation of beds at Leeds General Infirmary was an issue in June, 1920, according to an article in *The British Medical Journal* for that month. A Faculty meeting described it as "a highly contentious matter", but members were prepared to make concessions in talks with the Ministry of Pensions.

"During the years of the war the division of the beds between the various departments has been modified and obscured by many circumstances. Thus, on the outbreak of the struggle a request came from the War Office for accommodation for 115 wounded soldiers, and this was afterwards increased to 135. A ward which is usually kept as an emergency ward was at once put in commission and the large out-patient waiting hall was converted and used for the accommodation of patients, much of the out-patient work being relegated to temporary centres near the infirmary.

"In passing, it may be mentioned that 4,918 soldiers from convoys were dealt with in the infirmary, and in this way the pressure on the Second Northern General Hospital was lessened. The admission of soldiers came to an end in 1919, but beginning in 1918 and still continuing there has been a yearly admission of discharged soldiers, who are being sent by some one or other of the authorities acting under the Ministry of Pensions. The figures for 1918, 1919 and 1920 were respectively 346, 353 and 283, and it is hoped that the numbers will dwindle and this call on the infirmary will disappear, except possibly for a small number of special cases sent for investigation.

"The buildings of the Second Northern General Hospital are being used for pensioners, and this would appear to make further demands on the infirmary unnecessary, except, perhaps, for very special cases…"

> In March he (Major Alfred Hardwick, Regimental Medical Officer) was given a two-week pass, long enough to go all the way back home to see his family. While he was there he bought two ferrets… the ferrets couldn't have made a better start… bombing out of their cages, they returned to place the giant rat dead at Hardwick's feet. It was better than getting a medal. From then on, the ferrets boarded in their own dugout in a nearby shell hole and were released daily. They never failed to find their prey, with thirty-five being the record. (From *Wounded* by Emily Mayhew)

A CASE OF DERMOGRAPHISM

(From the Neurological Department, 2nd Northern General Hospital, Leeds)

Pte W, aged 20, was admitted to this hospital in May, 1919, with a gunshot wound of the right upper arm and ulnar nerve injury.

His attention had first been drawn to the ease with which his skin whealed three months previously when, while washing himself, he received a slap on his chest from a fellow patient, which was followed by a raised impression of the hand. Since then he noticed that a tight shirt wristband, a tight collar or bandage would cause a raised wheal on the underlying skin.

The words in the photograph (DERMO GRAPH) were traced by moderately firm pressure with a blunt piece of wood. The urticarial wheals took about three minutes to develop fully. As they rose they were at first uniformly pink, but finally were white and bloodless in the centre with a bright pink border. They subsided in from half to three hours, according to the pressure used to create them, and vanished rather more quickly from the arms than from the back and chest. There was no itching of the skin. The readiness of the patient to sweat on slight exertion furnishes further evidence of vasomotor instability.

The patient exhibited no signs of hysteria, and examination revealed nothing else abnormal either in the nervous system or elsewhere, except that, although a Yorkshireman, he spoke quickly, almost to the point of clipping and slurring his words, and unintelligibility.

His family history furnished no sign of neurotic heredity, his parents, brothers and sisters being quite healthy and, as the patient knew, none presented this phenomenon of factitious urticaria.

The patient himself stated that he had always been healthy, was classified A1 on joining the army, and during his six and a half months in France suffered from nothing until he was wounded. The only other feature of interest is that two months previous to his first noticing the condition he was in hospital in London, and whilst lying in the anaesthetic room waiting for some operation, an ether bottle exploded and caught fire. He assisted the nurse to extinguish the flames, and was rather scared and tremulous afterwards. He was anaesthetized, however, and the surgical procedure was carried out. There were no ill effects on recovering from the anaesthetic.

I have to thank Lieut-Colonel C E Ligertwood, DSO, the administrator of this hospital, for permission to record the case.

H S Carter, MB, ChB Captain RAMC (SR)

This piece appeared in *The British Medical Journal*, 31 January 1920

THE BLUE BAND

The magazine of the Second Northern General Hospital ran from September 1919 to January 1920 and was named in reference to the blue hospital uniform. There were five issues, all of them steered by Captain Hartley S. Carter, its literary editor. It was something of an improvement on the previous magazine, with its less-than-snappy name of *Journal of Leeds Territorial Hospitals*. The first issue went on sale ten months after the Armistice at a price of tuppence (two old pennies) for patients and threepence (a small silver coin) for anybody else.

"We are a small township of something like 2500 souls set down in the midst of a far larger city," wrote Carter in the first editorial. "It is incredible that we should live from month to month with no organ to chronicle our doings, the humour, pathos and endless variety that constitute the life of a great hospital; and that we should have no means of representing ourselves to the citizens of Leeds amongst whom we live." He goes on to thank all the willing helpers who have made it possible, urges local firms and tradesmen to buy advertising space and points out that the magazine should be useful for "wounded, disabled and ex-servicemen on the look-out for new careers". I imagine that the editor and many of the contributors would have written articles previously for the publications of various public schools, but the tone is not overwhelmingly elitist, in spite of the classical references to be found here and there, and not entirely aimed at the officers' mess, the officers in this case being highly trained medical men.

Carter is self-indulgent, but this is understandable: he seems to have been very well-read, and could perhaps have gone on to publish fiction or poetry himself, to join the company of many other literary medics, like Tobias Smollett or Anton Chekhov. His two-part article on the poetry of his hero, Rudyard Kipling, is spread over two issues and long for a magazine like this, but it is perceptive, intelligent and generally well-done. Unsurprisingly, he admires the way that Kipling probes into the thinking of the typical private soldier (remarked upon by many others, including the Russian poet Yevgeny Yevtushenko) but writes that his later work was "spoiled by smug-faced Jingoism", adding that Kipling's early poems will survive because "there is a catchiness and a swing about many of them which was then quite refreshing in English poetry". Carter's main passions, though, were pathology and bacteriology.

THE EDITOR AT HOME.

Although he dominated, there were also news and sports editors with less flair for the job. Contributors tended to sign off with initials rather than names, or use pen-names like Nemo, which means 'no man' in Latin. Dark, soldierly humour, heavy satire, bland reporting of official events, advice on practical matters like pension entitlements, and poetry were features of each issue. There are mysterious cheeky references here and there, often involving coming back late from town or amorous adventures, and one or two surprising items, like the series of translations of poems in Charles Baudelaire's *Les Fleurs du Mal*. The magazine also gives invaluable insights and information to any local historian prepared to trawl through it. Copies are available in Leeds Central Library.

> The popular writer H C McNeile, using the pen name 'Sapper', created the fictional character Bulldog Drummond in 1920. Described as "detective, patriot, hero and gentleman" on the cover of the eponymous novel, our hero is a veteran of the trenches, brutalized by his wartime experiences and bored with his post-war lifestyle – just like many of the readers.

SELECTIONS FROM THE BLUE BAND

Sonnet to an empty beer-bottle

I see thee by the roadside, cast away;
The cork that checked the flow of nectar gone;
The body sad vacuity; alone;
Thy useless label fading in decay.
I needs must stop at this, thy latter day
And ruminate thy history that is done.
Did'st once hold good beer that dost now hold none
Or but a watery liquor? Did'st thou stay
A wanderer's thirst, or, one of many, die
In mad carousal, Bacchanalian shame,
Or swill the belly of a lout, beef-crammed?
What strange fate made thee in the gutter lie?
I will approach and read thy honoured name.
Non-alcoholic ale! Well I'll be damned.

(Anon)

Little Miss Muffet,
Sat on a buffet,
And talked to an officer swell;
But Matron, who'd missed her,
Appeared as he kissed her,
And Nurse Muffet got –
Soundly rated!

There was a young damsel of Tottenham
Whose manners she had quite forgotten 'em;
In spite of the mockings
She took off her stockings
Because she was feeling too hot in 'em.

Song of the R.A.F.

The R.A.F. claims the foremost place –
Although with humble piety!
You'll own in dress it sets the pace,
If only for variety!
You can breakfast in your old khaki,
Lunch in a tunic of the R.F.C.,
In navy take your girl to tea,
And dine in your new blue-grey, sir!

You may fly a Camel or a Sopwith Pup,
But 'ware lest a Hun should nail you,
For you can't get out and crank her up
If once her engines fail you.
Just put her down and plane to earth,
Swoop through Archies for all you're worth,
And trust to luck to find a good berth,
Or you may give a job to the padre.

Flying by night on a lone patrol
With death around you lurking,
Needs men who are true and strong of soul
If there's to be no shirking.
So all who admire true bravery,
And the men who fly by land and sea,
Just drink this toast, good sirs, with me –
Here's to the British Airmen!
The Airmen! The Airmen!
Here's to the British Airmen!

The Masseuse
(after 'Roses of Picardy')

She is standing by her battery
Dour and grim, whilst her patient sighs;
She is piling on the 'lectric
In spite of pleading eyes;
And a wail breaks through the silence
Begging mercy from Heaven above;
She calmly turns on more current –
Inverse ratio of her love.

Chorus:

Batteries are working in harmony
In those torture rooms B3 and 4;
Patients are writhing in agony.
(The masseuse thinks 'tis what they are for)
And their mem'ries may fail with the flow of time
And their case sheets may fade and decay,
But they'll never forget till eternity
The torments they suffered each day.

Tinkle, tinkle, little pension,
Wealth beyond our comprehension,
Ten bob for the wife's new hat,
Six to make my baby fat,
Leaves a pound for me to spend –
Hope this life will never end!

Chronicles of Beckette
By the Scribe that Dwelleth in Beckette

And lo, it came to pass on a certain day,
That there were some in the House of Beckette,
Who said,
Behold, let us go down into the city
For our hearts be merry and we would rejoice.
Yea, unto the tavern let us go
And drink and eat and be glad
And comfort ourselves with flagons.
But alas
When they had come to the gates of the place
There issued forth one who cried, saying
Behold the band of blue which is upon thine
arm!
It shall be made fast.
Yea verily, it shall be sewn round about
So that no man may move it
And until this be done,
None may pass from the House of Beckette.
And because of this there was much sorrow
And wailing and gnashing of teeth,
For they who would make merry
Were filled with exceeding great sadness
At the thought of that thing.

(Short extract)

The Ideal
(Translated from Baudelaire's L'Idéal)

Vignetted beauties, pale coquettes,
Frail products of a world's decline,
With buskinned feet and castanets,
Will never charm a heart like mine.

I know Garvani's pallid dolls;
She does not flitter among those
Whose beauty fills the hospitals;
My ideal flower, my crimson rose!

For darkling women I repine;
A crime-scorched soul like Macbeth's wife;
- A dream of Aeschylus divine,
'Tis such as thou shalt charm my life!

Or brooding Night – whose sinuous charms
Great Angelo gave fire to be
Love's burden for Titanic arms –
Queen of them all shall be for me!

Nabbed

Raise a grin,	Carry on	The high jump
What a lark!	Through the murk.	On next day.
Coming in	Ce n'est pas bon –	Got the hump –
Beckett Park	Wiring work	Five days pay –
After dark	While foes lurk.	Oh I say!
Quiet climb	Can it be?	No khaki
Through the wire	Is it aught?	And no pass,
After time –	Th' enemy!	Woe is me!
Torn attire,	Awful thought,	Lost the brass,
Raising ire.	We are caught!	And the lass!

A lance corporal's confession

…My first impressions of the 2nd Northern general Hospital were far from rosy. In the first three weeks as a general-duty orderly I cleaned almost every piece of brasswork with a piece of old shirt, aided by the liquid called "Brasso" from A wards to G wards – the extension was not built at that time. My domestic training being thus completed, I was chosen as policeman to guard the gate which crowns Church Wood Avenue. Four hours on and eight hours off was the rule. It was an acknowledged fact that , in 1915 when Captains ---- and ---- had passed through the gate, the policeman on duty was quite safe until the morning, as these two gentlemen were always the last to arrive back home. Only once during my policemanship did one of these gentlemen fail me.

When all had returned home to roost, it was the custom of the gateman to tie the gate together with a slip-knot, and then tie himself to a certain spot and sleep for the remainder of his tour of duty, returning about five minutes before the arrival of the relief. I made no exception to the rule and confess that on each and every occasion it was a great success. Patients at this time were not allowed out, and I should imagine that the policeman now on that gate has not such a "bobby's job" as I had when in his shoes, almost four years ago. If the slip-knot had slipped and had been found on the ground, the policeman would automatically have realized he was "on the peg" and for the "high jump". One is thankful to know that one is still alive after committing a crime the penalty for which is death, and that before dawn.

How often have I looked across Jordan? A Clerk in Holy Orders told me at that time that he thought of and prayed for me during my night watches. It is not the duty of a policeman to be bribed, but 300 cigarettes and a fair amount of fruit was an average taking between the hours of 2 and 4 on visiting afternoons. Having completed a month on the police, I was placed on the staff, and ultimately became a lance corporal…

On one occasion I was hauled up for an unforgivable crime. The occasion was when the low lights, blinds down and Zeppelin fear orders were first issued, and no less than half the R.A.M.C. unit were brought before the Company Officer for not drawing the blinds in their rooms. For this crime the whole host was given C.B. for 24 hours…

By "Not Nemo"

Private Taylor's reminiscences

The lady was very kind, also interested, and Private Taylor, the permanent bed patient, felt that he had a sympathetic listener, so he gave some of his reminiscences of the firing line. She also had cakes and cigarettes and our hero felt it was up to him to do his best and give value for money. After describing how he got his tenth wound-stripe, and receiving thereby another packet of Gold Flake, he decided it was time to give the grand finale.

"So running across No Man's Land," he said, "I came across a party of Germans, fifty strong, who attacked me with machine guns, hand grenades and poison gas. Finding I could not bayonet them quickly enough, I pulled my lanyard off my arm, made a lassoo, and in a trice those poor Jerries were trussed up like fowls. I had then to simply drag them across to our lines and deliver them up to headquarters, receiving from a grateful country the V.C., M.M. and O.B.E."

On coming to the end of this alarming series of accidents, Taylor looked expectantly at the lady, but she, looking neither to the right or the left, dropped her remaining valuables and fled the place. She has never been heard of since.

Going to the pictures?

"Going to the pictures?" To the unsophisticated this would no doubt sound a very common question. But to the wounded Tommy it can mean only one thing on a certain day – a visit to the operating theatre.

Practically every inmate of a military hospital has played leading man in one of these fascinating dramas, which begin and end in thick darkness. One peculiar thing about them is that they cannot be described with any degree of coherence. They are vague dreams of horror and magic.

There is much preparation for these great days. The expectant Tommy is well washed and cleaned so that he may appear at his best; also he must have a good rest before he sets off on his journey. The great drawback however is that he is not allowed any meals on the day of adventure. It is considered that the food mortals eat would be useless when he passes to the ethereal realm. In fact this is the ideal land where food is not needed.

At the appointed hour the chariot appears, the patient prepares to depart, and the last farewells are said. He is consulted as to his fancies in wreaths and crosses, and a collection is suggested in order to erect a suitable tombstone.

After these preliminaries the victim is hurried into an anteroom, where he sees many strange and weird instruments. With a determined look on its face a white figure approaches, and the unfortunate one finds himself pinned down with a suffocating mask over his face. In a few moments all is over, and he lies, a still figure, on the slab… and then a sense of quickly moving events is passing through his brain, then quietness, and he opens his eyes with a start. Nothing matters however, and he closes them again.

Then he becomes conscious that something is biting and gnawing at him. Thought comes, and with it a realization that he is groaning and crying out. Someone, dimly familiar, is bending over him telling him it is all over now, and he is back again in the ward. He allows time for this to sink in, then a feeling of great thankfulness comes to him to think that he has pulled through once more. The 'pictures' are over.

By Nemo

For men about to be discharged

For every town or district there is a Local War Pensions Committee, or one of their representatives. These committees are supposed to be able to give you any information you desire and all necessary help.

For the first month after discharge you will draw 27/6 per week. This is given to you in the hospital, on the morning of your discharge, when you will receive four postal drafts, each value 27/6. These are to be cashed weekly at any post office.

When you have got your ticket

Enquire for one of the 1800 branches of the "Comrades of the Great War" and join up again.

Mothers of deceased soldiers

The Select Committee on Pensions is again sitting. Further evidence is to be called, and it is expected that the Committee will take up the case of the awards to mothers of deceased soldiers. It has been suggested that the 5s. pension should be increased to 7s. 6d and the 15s. pension to £1.

A Hint to Limbless Men

Most limbless men have no information regarding their stump-socks and arm-mitts. These are supplied with your first artificial limb. You should receive 6 stump-socks or 4 arm-mitts for each leg or arm, from the hospital. Afterwards you can get supplies renewed every six months but only if you apply to your L.W.P.C. (Information kindly supplied by Mrs Coupland's Committee)

Dental Treatment

Many pensioners have asked whether it is at all possible for them to receive free dental treatment. Free dental treatment can only be given if the condition is due to or aggravated by service. In every case where treatment is applicable, the man should apply to his L.W.P.C. who have power to authorize the necessary treatment.

Training

If you cannot return to your old work and wish to be trained, under the Government scheme for a new job, apply at once on your return home to your L.W.P.C. who should be able to give you all necessary information.

Is that rabbit too frisky?

One is sometimes in doubt as to whether the last consignment of freshly trapped rabbits shipped by the local poulterer is not more useful for rat poison than for rissoles. A decision may be most expeditiously arrived at by taking one of the defunct mammals, and, after donning a gas-mask, pricking it in the most prominent region of the abdomen with one of the wife's hatpins. If the suspected carcase collapses with a loud hiss, and you experience a choking sensation in the chest, combined with signs of rapid exhaustion of the contents of the gas-mask, transfer the body to the furrier's or deposit it on a neighbour's rubbish-heap.

Oysters

Patients are urged, before eating oysters, to discover whether they are polluted. In order to do this, the whites of the oysters' eyes should be examined.

Shell Shock

For the benefit of those suffering from Shell Shock, we are able to report that the following definition on the subject has just been published – "It is really a molecular abnormality of the nervous system, characterized by abnormal reactions to ordinary stimuli." Will those concerned please note?

Cricket

The establishment of a cricket team, composed entirely of patients – wounded men, with various disabilities – who have consistently displayed such good "form" that out of 21 matches played this season, they have won 15, and lost only 6 – is perhaps as unique as may be found in the annals of our national summer game, with all its glorious uncertainties.

It is not possible, within the scope of this brief resumé, to give a detailed analysis of the matches played, but from the following results, it will be seen that the Hospital team is to be congratulated on its performance against no mean opponents. (Results of matches with Leeds University, Headingley, YMCA, Hunslet Adults, Beckett Park College, RAF, Kirkstall, RAMC (Staff), Mr Dibbs XI and Lofthouse Park teams follow)

Football

The Hospital team played its first game on September 10th, when they defeated the R.A.M.C. by eight goals to two. With a little hard practice the patients should be able to raise a very good team, some of the players showing remarkably good talent. As may be indicated by the score, the game against the R.A.M.C. was rather a one-sided affair, the patients keeping the ball in their opponents' half for the greater part of the game.

The team is entered for the Leeds Hospital Cup Competition and plays in the first round against Headingley Wesleyans on the ground of the latter team.

Boxing

The sporting instincts of the patients were well gratified on the night of the 17th ult., by an attractive Boxing display, organized by Capt. Michie, Capt. Scott and Dr. Friend… a regulation ring kindly lent by Mr. Foster Thompson was fitted up… Quite a number of Stars in the local Boxing firmament appeared in exhibition bouts of sparring, notably the famous Spike Robson, Louis Ruddick, Young Fox and Myers Stringer…

Smoking Concert

The Warrant Officers, Staff Sergeants and Sergeants of the 2nd Northern General Hospital entertained their friends to a most enjoyable Social And Smoking Concert in the Mess Room of Macaulay Hostel on Friday the 10th ult. Among the Officers of the Administrative Staff who accepted invitations to be present were Capt. Graham, R.A.M.C (Registrar), Capt. Michie (Quartermaster), Capt. Carter, R.A.M.C. and the Rev. R. Ward, C.F. The Chair was taken by the President of the Mess (R.S.M. Mehan) supported by Q.M.S. Oxley and Q.M.S. Steele A musical programme gave much pleasure, and Messrs. Holroyd and Matkin proved themselves delightful entertainers, as did the Misses Beevers and Wadsworth, not to mention the efforts of Sergeants Sloper and Dale.

Sacred Concert

Under the auspices of the Y.M.C.A. a sacred concert was given on the afternoon of the 26th ult. Tea was provided for the many patients present, and the programme was given by members of the Leeds Philharmonic Society. Miss Annie Windsor as soprano soloist gave a fine rendering of "O Divine Redeemer" and the items contributed by Mrs. Ambler (Contralto), Mr. A.J. Burnet (Tenor) and Mr. Gaunt Lee (Bass), were each well applauded. The accompanist was Mrs. H.P. Atkinson.

The Rev. J.W. Grindell, of the Brunswick Wesleyan Circuit, addressed the men on the "Fullness of Life". His message was that the greatest prize in "life" was the development of a good character; that all men started equal in the sweet innocence of childhood, and that each made the choice of the good and bad in life. The address was much appreciated.

Leeds Choral Society

The Matron is pleased to acknowledge the gift of three pounds for limbless patients, from an anonymous donor in Harrogate; also concert tickets for patients and staff from the Secretaries of the Leeds Choral Society. Thanks are also due to the Committee of the Brunswick Club for their generosity in entertaining fifty patients to a tea and concert, and the provision of motor-charabancs for the conveyance of the men.

Annual Ball

The annual regimental ball of the R.A.M.C. …took place on the 12th ult…….in the large assembly hall… A large number of guests accepted invitations, there being about 400 present. The M.C.s were Staff-Sergeants F.E. Smith and G.N. Sprittles.

Christmas

The traditions of the festive season were well observed at Beckett Park, although Santa Claus failed to put in an appearance. Wards had, apparently, vied with each other in their decorative schemes, which, without exception, were exceedingly tasteful. As was anticipated, many convalescents, including a proportion of the staff, availed themselves of the opportunity of leave, consequently there were, approximately, but 400 (most of whom were bed-patients) present to enjoy the fare provided. Xmas Day was ushered in to the tuneful carol singing of the surpliced choir of St. Michael's Church Headingley, and no effort was spared by the matron and her staff, aided by the Ladies Committee under Mrs. Coupland, to make the occasion a very happy one for all in hospital. The result was that many are left with pleasant recollections of Xmas Day at Beckett Park, especially that of the Dinner, which by common assent, was excellent… A Concert Party provided by the Lady Mayoress of Leeds entertained the men in several wards, and on Boxing Day there was a Concert and Picture Show in the Recreation Hall.

The Cheero Boys

The Cheero Troupe have given two concerts during the past month. Four members – Privates Fenton, Fryer, Hartley and Rostron – were amongst the draft, which went to Blackpool on Easter Monday. To them and to Staff-Sergt. Beck and Private Lindsay, who still remain, the hospital is much indebted. For more than a year they have been a constant source of pleasure. A hastily-arranged concert on Easter Eve served as a farewell, and the Recreation Hall was crowded with members of staff and patients. (From *The Journal,* April 1918)

Hospital band

The Hospital Band was given leave to play in City Square on three days during "The Cruiser Week". In spite of the loss of various members through discharge they acquitted themselves well. Private Hazel was kindly given a conductor's baton by the Matron. New members are now wanted.

The Male Voice Choir have given three concerts at Beckett Park, East Leeds and Killingbeck. They have suffered a great loss by the departure of Private Fenton, who had acted as conductor and given much skill and care to their training. At the Cheero farewell concert a fountain pen was presented to him as a recognition of his services, by the members.

The usual concerts by "Music in War Time" and Mr. Clifford Bowling's Party have taken place. Mr G. Parker, of the Chapels Royal, has kindly promised to sing on April 9th. Lectures have been given by Prof. Parker and by the Rev. E.A. Prince, C.F. "Pictures" have had a crowded attendance and have been well shewn by Corpl. Scott.

There were large congregations on Good Friday and Easter Day. On the evening of Good Friday the members of the Philharmonic Society kindly gave a performance of Stainer's "Crucifixion".

Pierrots

Weynington Ward were provided musical evenings by Miss Pollard and Mr. Hepburn's parties, while Mr. Pickard and his party entertained the men in Sturdee and Frobisher Wards. Miss Varley and others gave a programme that was much enjoyed in Hawke Ward and the "Y.M." and later the "Chapeltown Pierrots" under Miss Clarke gave a very fine entertainment in the "Y.M."

Fruit and cigarettes

Under the Leeds War Hospital entertainment scheme (of which Mr. Clifford Bowling is the secretary), concerts have been given at Killingbeck, Stainbeck, Armley House and Beckett Park during the month. On the 6th ult., Miss Black was the hostess in Beatty Ward, where a tea and concert (including fruit and cigarettes) were provided for the patients. The artistes included the Misses Ivy Mellor, Violet Black, and Porritt, also Messrs. Matkin, Buck, Freeman, Holroyd and McDougall, with Mr Greenwood at the piano. Miss Porritt was well received, it being her first appearance as a public singer.

Orphanage children

On Tuesday the 9th September, at the invitation of Mr. Robert Brown, a party of some twenty-four boys and girls, ranging in age from seven to twelve years, from the Bramhope National Orphanage School, entertained the hospital in the evening with a programme of songs and choruses, tableaux, and exercises in drill and skipping. The children at once got right to the heart of the patients, who applauded them vociferously, and it was apparent that the little artistes reciprocated the pleasure they were giving to others. The boys showed to advantage in a delightful action song in "A hunting we will go", while the Misses Mabel Butters and Frances Searle brought down the house with a most clever exhibition of skipping. The careful training of the children reflects credit on the Principal – Miss Moon, and her assistant, Miss Denison.

Future prospects

Most patients after 1918 must have been very concerned about their future employment prospects, and they were the targets of many advertisers who knew about their fears and aspirations. 'Pelman Courses' feature several times, wordy half pages with titles like 'Brain Magic' and sentences like "In fact it is clearly proved that Pelmanism means that in a few weeks, by practicing for a few minutes daily, anyone can open up the road to fortune, success, and even wealth and fame." Pelmanism was a system of memory training, taught by correspondence, which could allegedly cure forgetfulness, phobias and procrastination. Other 'betterment' advertisers included Berlitz School of Languages, Pitman's (Shorthand Rapid Course, How to become a qualified accountant etc), Metropolitan College, St Alban's (Specialised Postal Training) and Bennett College, Sheffield, for which "Students may if they prefer pay by instalments. All text books provided free".

Educational tours, promoted by the Army Education Scheme, involved small parties of patients who visited workshops and factories, for example the Public benefit Boot Factory, Johnson's Soap Works, *Yorkshire Post* printing works and Hepworth's Clothing Factory.

Trips outside the city were sponsored by various organisations and firms, for example the staff of the Leeds Post Office, who made it possible for twenty-five patients to be "conveyed by motor to Bardsey… the route taken being via Arthington, Harewood and East Keswick. The beautifully fine weather added charm to the early autumn scenery of the countryside. On arrival at Bardsey, the men, chiefly limbless cases, found an excellent tea provided for them by the hostess of The Bingley Arms (Mrs Benchley), which was given gratuitously by this lady, who states that she will always be pleased to entertain the men." On another occasion, a charabanc-load dined at the Marquis of Granby in Knaresborough.

The Debating Society attracted about forty people at a time, all of them sitting in E1 – the Education Office. Subjects included The League of Nations, Divorce Laws, "Our modern necessity, the cinema" and Coal Nationalisation.

The Pictures

References to 'the pictures' and films are many, because the industry had such a strong grip on so many imaginations. Hollywood had already become the main centre for the English-speaking world, and a growing number of people knew about Charlie Chaplin's Little Tramp with his baggy trousers and bowler hat. Projection equipment was brought into Beckett Park frequently, and matinee shows at the Headingley Picture House in Cottage Road (opened 1912) were free to wounded men and half price for soldiers in uniform. Some of the silent films shown there to piano accompaniment are still obtainable, but I suspect that most of them have been lost, or destroyed: if they were on a nitrate base they might sometimes have burned up in the cinema, touched off by the heat of the projector lamp. Seven films were on the programme for November 1919: The Safety Curtain, Inside the Lines, Pauline Frederick's The Woman on the Index, A Pair of Silk Stockings, Queen of Hearts, Tom Mix in Treat 'em Rough and The Great Love. Prices of admission were 9d (ninepence) and 1/3 (one and threepence) including tax. Tom Mix in his huge white Stetson was the first cowboy megastar, appearing in hundreds of films, mainly silent. Type in 'Tom Mix' on Youtube today and you get 'Tom Jones Mix'.

Things we would like to know

This was the title of a column which appeared in every issue.

Why the "Gay Lothario" of "curtain fame" now avoids his former rendezvous.
The exact nature of the attraction Adel has for the V.A.D.s.

Whether there was any addition to the "Lab" as the result of the Keystones recent inspection of the wire, and why the garden barrow was employed.

If the gentleman of the staff who kissed the lady with his pipe in his mouth is not more in love with "My Lady Nicotine".

Whether the N.C.O. who frequents the Roundhay pool has successfully taught the lady the art of oarsmanship, and whether this can be done from the bottom of the boat.

Whether there are not other advantages in sleeping on a verandah besides that of having a good view of the garden.

Has the potato peeler got the "strike fever"?

When may we expect a revival in Jazz Band music?

Should Chaplains flirt?

> I will not leave a corner of my consciousness covered up, but saturate myself with the strange and extraordinary new conditions of this life, and it will all refine itself into poetry later on. **Isaac Rosenberg** (Killed near Arras, April 1918)

ARTISTS AND ENTERTAINERS

According to contemporary reports in the local press, personal accounts and photographs, Beckett Park patients were visited very regularly – by relatives, friends and colleagues of course, but also by groups from mills and factories, sporting clubs, school children, choirs, concert parties and musicians. Most of them came with gifts - mainly fruit and cigarettes. This was in addition to the garden parties, sporting fixtures and other open events held in the grounds which provided opportunities for hospital inmates and members of the public to mingle. Projection equipment was available in the large YMCA hut to show the latest films to patients unable to visit the Headingley Picture House.

The few available brief reviews and commentaries on visiting entertainers are all polite, thankful and rather bland. It would have been bad form to criticize the great efforts made by well-meaning civilians too openly or negatively, though some cartoons and postcards of the time, not connected specifically with Beckett Park, depict bed patients making comical or sarcastic comments about those who have intruded upon them.

Harry Clifford Bowling, born 1869 in Heckmondwike, Yorkshire, was the secretary to the Leeds War Hospital Entertainments Committee. He was a solicitor who specialised in bankruptcy cases, and according to papers of the Leeds Philosophical and Literary Society deposited in the Brotherton Library (in 1975) he was concerned about the requirements of the government's Entertainment Tax of 1916 and its implications for what his concert party did for invalid soldiers at all the Leeds war hospitals and convalescent homes. He was also one of the secretaries of the Leeds Philharmonic Society, some of whose members came up to the hospital to sing extracts from various oratorios, or to provide John Stainer's *Crucifixion* at Easter. He was an opera lover and a friend of the leading conductor Sir Thomas Beecham for many years : a printed score of Puccini's *La Bohème* which belonged to him was auctioned online in 2013 with the following in its flyleaf : 'Leeds Grand Theatre 23 Nov 1935. This book is a friend in need – thanks to my other friend Clifford Bowling, Thomas Beecham". It is also signed by the soprano Lisa Perli, Beecham's mistress. The repertoire of Bowling's concert party remains unknown, but it is unlikely to have been mainly classical music.

Classical music was certainly brought to the hospital, and it can be assumed that it was appreciated by many. Anyone performing on a Leeds platform or stage throughout the war would have at least been told about the possibilities of spending some time with the wounded. The pianist Frederick Dawson came to Beckett Park, and I like to imagine that the well-known local pianist Charles Wilkinson, father of Dorothy (see her story) contributed something as well.

Carrie Tubb, a famous operatic soprano up from the Leeds Grand Theatre, sang at Beckett Park, perhaps in a ward or two, but there is no record of what it was. It is unlikely to have been Wagner, even though she had become famous at Covent Garden and at the London Proms for her performances in his operas. According to the BBC Proms Archive, she sang pieces from *Götterdämmerung* and *Tristan und Isolde* in 1916, 1917 and 1918, and from Tannhäuser in 1919. There was a Leeds connection, of sorts: in 1915 she was with baritone Robert Radford and the Leeds Festival Chorus in Bach's Mass in B minor at the Queen's Hall in London under Henri Verbrugghen with the London Symphony Orchestra. I would guess that she gave the patients something from Mendelssohn's *Elijah,* which she had sung for the Gramophone Company (HMV) a few years previously: beneath the crackles her lovely voice can be heard. She also sang for soldiers at the front. In spite of widespread propaganda which demonized the Germans, music by German composers seems to have appeared regularly on programmes, despite some (doomed) recommendations that it should be avoided.

Opera singer Carrie Tubb

At St Chad's church, which is very close to Beckett Park, a search through the yellowing pages of the thin parish magazines of 1914 – 1918 reveals that *Brahms's German Requiem* was performed every year by the choir, which was aided by reinforcements from other choirs. I am sure they sang it in its English translation. The normal way of dealing with the Germans and the German names which were embarrassingly still amongst the British in the war years was to either Anglicise or change them. Thus members of the Royal Family became Windsors, Battenburgs became Mountbattens, German Shepherd Dogs became Alsatians, and dachshunds got kicked around. All over Yorkshire, brass bands adapted their uniforms, many of them originally based on Bavarian ones.

There appears to be no record of the actors who visited Beckett Park, but they certainly did so, because Leeds with its theatres –the Hippodrome, the Empire Palace (now Harvey Nichols), the City Varieties and the Grand – was a major part of the touring circuit. Surely one of them was Queenie Gwynne. She starred in the pantomime *Cinderella* at the Grand Theatre on Boxing Day, 1917. According to the reviewer in the *Yorkshire Post,* "the capacious Grand Theatre could not comfortably hold more" because of the many soldiers home from leave, who were there with children, "the elders" and "boys home from school". "Miss Queenie Gwynne can also be assured that she has passed the opera-glass scrutiny with honour, and she is now at liberty to go ahead and exercise that winsome disposition which one knows to be within her gift. There was much approval of her musical appeal to Santa Claus to send, as the prime present for Christmas, her Daddy back from the front. The pretty consummation of this request was cleverly enacted."

According to *Leeds in the Great War* (1923) the artists who visited the wounded in all of the war hospitals included "vocalists, instrumentalists, accompanists, elocutionists, dancers, comedians, ventriloquists, conjurors, mimics, jugglers, cartoonists, sword experts and other variety entertainers".

THE CHEERO BOYS

And he was attending that fancy-dress ball, mark you--not, like every other well-bred Englishman, as a Pierrot, but as Mephistopheles--this involving, as I need scarcely stress, not only scarlet tights but a pretty frightful false beard.

From *Right Ho Jeeves* by P G Wodehouse (1934)

A wardrobe of pierrot costumes seems to have been standard issue in hospitals for the wounded, judging from the photographs and references from all over the country. Beckett Park's pierrot troupe, or concert party – the terms are more or less interchangeable – was called the Cheero Boys, or the Cheeros. They were considered to be valuable aids for recovery because, funnily enough, they cheered people up, and consisted of a group of RAMC men from the lower ranks. Their shows in the YMCA hut were probably the most successful ones, and they were booked for concerts in other hospitals. It is not known if they were treading the boards in the war's first years, but they were certainly going strong at the end of it. George Sprittles pasted several photographs in his scrapbook, one of them marked with the date of their final performance at Easter 1918, on the evening before the members were ordered to a camp near Blackpool to prepare for the Middle East. Later, he added the photos of themselves they sent home from Palestine. They were wearing uniform shorts.

Pierrots with whitened faces and black skull-caps, dressed in baggy costumes with pom poms (usually black on white), increased in popularity as the twentieth century progressed. They first appeared on summer beaches at the end of the nineteenth century, the concept imported from France, and made the popular black-face minstrel shows of the time seem old-fashioned, though London's Metropolitan Police minstrels lasted until the 1930s. Pierrot troupes with names like

The Fol-de-Rols toured seaside towns in between the wars (see J B Priestley's *The Good Companions*) with their version of Variety, which had replaced music hall entertainment, and they were still doing so up to the Second World War. After that, their place in popular culture was taken by holiday camp entertainers like the Redcoats at Butlin's.

The theatrical ancestor of the Cheeros was the sad clown who never gets the soft-as-a-dove pretty girl (Columbina) in the Commedia del'Arte performances of sixteenth century Italy, but that was surely a faraway link, because the RAMC privates who pulled off the khaki and smeared on the greasepaint were essentially young men with a talent for raising a laugh who could also sing. On the other hand, one of Sprittles' photos shows some Cheero Boys in blue patients' uniforms peering at one of their number in a wig, dressed as a nurse, a Columbina. Scripts have not been found, and were probably pencil jottings, if they ever existed.

I imagine that they were consumers as well as producers, influenced by shows they had seen either before or during the war. One of the people they might have had in mind was Fred Karno, the London impresario who had once employed Charlie Chaplin and Stan Laurel before they were drawn to California, the man who is supposed to have invented the custard pie in the face gag. One of the songs associated with soldiers in the trenches is 'We are Fred Karno's Army' sung to the tune of 'The Church's One Foundation'. They might have watched the pierrots as children on a beach, sitting in the sand, too grown-up for the Punch and Judy. Or they might have been to the front and seen a concert party there.

Concert parties were commonplace in every regiment, performing when and where they could, at home and in France and Flanders. Francis Lewis in his reminiscences writes about being billeted in the strengthened cellar of a ruined house somewhere in France, where there was a supply of white wine, commenting "I think it was here that Lieutenant Wooster started the battalion concert party…" He goes on to describe how shows by the concert party alternated with boxing matches and adds that it "…was equipped with costumes and a stage and put on some excellent shows. Some of the highlights were 'Dixie' sung as a duet, 'Sergeant Sparrow with his Four Foot Ten Brigade' and Private Hayes, the comedian. Lieutenant Wooster had the knack of obtaining the necessary props." Original concert programmes (not for the Cheeros unfortunately) in Special Collections at the Brotherton Library show that names for concert parties included the Merry Tatlers, the Chequers, the Blue Dons, the Dominoes, the Empties, the Devil's Own Revue, the Gaieties, the Royal Sussex Entertainers, the Bric-a-Bracs and the National Theatre of the Front. They produced Christmas pantomimes like *Robinson Crusoe* and scenes from Shakespeare's *Henry V* along with the usual singing and joking. It was not all morale-boosting for battalion comrades: the wounded in hospitals (back in Blighty) were also visited. Women joined in as well: the nurses at Waverley Abbey Hospital in Surrey had a group called the Candy Dandy Girls.

A page from one of the programmes gives some idea of what could be done: a one-act play, written by Lieutenant McConnel for D Company of the Seventh City of London Battalion, was entitled The *Gazeka's Pearl.* The characters are Hortensio, a waiter (Corporal Ridgway), Lord Dammitt, the villain (Sergeant James), Bertram Strong, the hero (Corporal Mardorf) and Angelica Agglebitters, a stately person (Lieutenant McConnel). The scene is the Café des Gourmets. The programme adds these details: "Miss Agglebitters' gown is by Madame Delicia (Middlesex Street). Her gems (insured by Lockhart's Ltd for £300,000) are by the S.Purious Co Ltd., and her dinky bag is supplied by the R.Q.M.S." There is an orchestra as well: Corporal Hardy and Sergeant Gatward played violins, Second Lieutenant de Lavison the cello; Sergeant Drummer Dennison and Corporal Ward were flautists, Drummer Pursford was on drums and Private Adams played the trumpet. The programme ends with GOD SAVE THE KING.

One of the songs which must have been in the Cheeros' repertoire was *Roses of Picardy.* With its reference to the French province which includes the Somme battlefields, and its sentimental melancholy, it became wildly popular. The lyrics were by the songwriter and barrister Fred Weatherly (who was also responsible for *Danny Boy*) and the music was by Yorkshire-born violinist Haydn Wood, who made a fortune from sales of the sheet music during the war. Soon after its composition in 1916, Wood toured the country with his wife, the soprano Dorothy Court, performing it at the Hippodrome in Leeds in October, 1917. An audience in the YMCA hut at Beckett Park, or in one of the wards, can easily be imagined joining the Cheeros in the refrain:

Roses are shining in Picardy, in the hush of the silver dew,
Roses are flowering in Picardy, but there's never a rose like you!
And the roses will die with the summertime, and our roads may be far apart,
But there's one rose that dies not in Picardy!
'tis the rose that I keep in my heart!

Professionals regularly travelled out to the front to perform, often organized by Lena Ashford, famous on the West End stage, in conjunction with the Ladies Auxiliary Committee of the YMCA, the president of which was Princess Victoria of Schleswig-Holstein. Its 'Concert for the front' scheme was started in 1915, and the numbers of its shows multiplied quickly.

CIGARETTE CASE

Richard Wilcocks was phoned up by a Wakefield antiques dealer who had read a feature in the *Yorkshire Post* about research into the hospital. He offered to give this cigarette case to any descendant of Colour Quartermaster Sergeant G W Browning, who won it in 1918. The photo was taken by his secretary. No trace of Sergeant Browning has been discovered, but there is a brief mention of Douglas Longmate in the National Archives as a maker of artificial limbs. It is not known whether or not these were of the usual wooden kind.

Wooden prosthetics were heavy and often uncomfortable. They did not improve much during the War, in spite of the huge number of amputees, but lightweight ones made of aluminium alloys were coming into increasing use. The first one of these was designed by his younger brother Charles for WW1 aviator Marcel Desoutter, who lost a leg after his plane crashed at Hendon Aerodrome in 1912. Marcel was soon back in the air, equipped with a leg made from duralumin. The brothers later went into business, making artificial limbs.

HEADINGLEY LITFEST

Headingley LitFest 2014

Surviving

Celebrating the creative word in Headingley - and Headingley in the creative word

Headingley has connections with many writers: **Arthur Ransome** was born in Headingley, **J R R Tolkien** lived at 5 Holly Bank and also at 2 Darnley Road, West Park when he was reader in English Language at the University of Leeds from 1920 to 1925, **Alan Bennett** lived over a butcher's shop opposite the Three Horseshoes, now Royale Dry Cleaners, **George Orwell** used to stay in Estcourt Terrace with his stepsister and her husband Humpy Dakin, **T S Eliot's** mother-in-law lived in Weetwood Lane, **William Fryer Harvey** was brought up in Spring Bank, **Trevor Griffiths** lived just off Victoria Road on Winstanley Terrace, **Jon Silkin** edited STAND magazine from his flat at 144 Otley Road, **Sir Geoffrey Hill** lived in Shire Oak Road, **Peter Redgrove** lived in the area, **Wilson Barrett,** the charismatic manager of Leeds Grand Theatre lived in Beech Grove in the 1870s and television playwright **Kay Mellor** currently lives near the Hollies. This is just a small selection.

Our venues include the Heart Centre on Bennett Road, the New Headingley Club on St Michael's Road, friendly cafés like Lento and Mint on North Lane, historic local cinemas, Headingley Library, people's houses and sometimes the Howard Assembly Room in the city centre.

The seventh annual LitFest took place in March 2014. As usual it was organized by a small team of volunteers who met throughout the year. Headline guests at previous LitFest have included **Dame Beryl Bainbridge, Robert Barnard, Roger McGough, Ian McMillan, Kay Mellor, Blake Morrison, David Peace, George Szirtes and Hilary Spurling.**

THE VEDETTES

Photo by Lloyd Spencer

The launch of this book at the New Headingley Club on 21 March 2014 was followed by a play based on three of the stories in it – Robert Bass, Margaret Anna Newbould and Dorothy Wilkinson – together with poems and songs. The performers were the Vedettes – **Richard Wilcocks,** who wrote the script, and three MA students from the Performing Arts department at Leeds Metropolitan University, **Katharina Arnold, Charlotte Blackburn** and **Hannah Robinson.** 'Vedettes' was one of the nicknames for women in the VAD (Voluntary Aid Detachment). It also means 'rising stars' in modern French.

Headingley LitFest

www.headingleylitfest.org.uk • www.headingleylitfest.blogspot.com

Wartime Hospital at Beckett Park

www.headingleyhospital.org • headingleyhospital@gmail.com

Telephone: 0113 225 7397

SOURCES

Leeds Metropolitan University Archive – Sprittles Scrapbook, various artefacts

Liddle Collection, Brotherton Library, University of Leeds – Annie Storey,
Violet Trafford-Towers, Leonard Rooke, concert parties, concert programmes

National Archives, Kew Imperial War Museum – matrons Jessie Hills and Euphemia Innes,
Lt. Leonard Rooke

Imperial War Museum, London – Francis Lewis, West Riding Territorial Force, Doctors in the
Great War, Hospital Ship Formosa

Leeds Central Library – copies of *The Blue Band*, newspapers (*Yorkshire Post, Evening Post,
Leeds Mercury, Leeds Citizen*) from 1914 – 1918

Thackray Medical Museum – autograph book of Nurse J Campbell, War Surgery,
Sir Berkeley Moynihan

Bibliography

Back to Activity by Means of Desoutter Artificial Limbs by E R Desoutter 1938

City of Leeds Training College. Continuity and Change 1907 – 2007 Edited by Lori Beckett
(Leeds Metropolitan University ISBN 978-0-9555017-4-6) First published 2007

Doctors in the Great War by Ian R Whitehead (Pen and Sword Books 978-1783461745) 2013

Goddamn This War! (Putain de Guerre!) by Jacques Tardi and Jean-Pierre Verney,
translated by Helge Dascher (Fantagraphics 978-1606995822) 2013

Leeds in the Great War, A Book of Remembrance by William Herbert Scott
(Leeds Libraries and Arts Committee) 1923

Leeds Pals by Laurie Milner (Leo Cooper ISBN 0 85052 335 4) 1991

Testament of Youth by Vera Brittain (Virago Press 0–86068-035-5)
First published by Victor Gollancz in 1933

The Beauty and the Sorrow. An Intimate History of the First World War by Peter Englund,
Translated by Peter Graves (Profile Books 978-1-84668-343-5)
First published in Great Britain 2011

The Great Silence: 1918-1920 Living in the Shadow of the Great War by Juliet Nicholson
(John Murray 978-0719562570) 2010

The Great War: July 1, 1916: The First Day of the Battle of the Somme
by Joe Sacco (W W Norton & Co 978-0393088809) 2013

The Making of Modern Britain From Queen Victoria to V.E. Day by Andrew Marr (Macmillan ISBN 978–0-230-70942-3) 2009

The Roses of No Man's Land by Lyn Macdonald (Penguin ISBN 0 – 14 – 017866 – X) First published by Michael Joseph in 1980

The West Riding Territorials in the Great War by Laurie Magnus (Kegan Paul, Trench, Trubner & Co) 1920

War Surgery From Firing Line To Base by B Hughes and H S Barnes (Bailliere, Tindall and Cox) 1918

Wounded, From Battlefield to Blighty 1914 – 1918 by Emily Mayhew (Bodley Head ISBN 9781847922618) 2013

Selected online sources

www.ancestry.co.uk, (Family and military histories)

http://www.ramc-ww1.com/ RAMC in the Great War

en.wikipedia.org,

http://libcudl.colorado.edu/wwi/pdf/i71178107.pdf
British Medicine in the War 1914 – 1917
London: The British Medical Association 1917

http://history.amedd.army.mil/booksdocs/wwi/VolXIPtI/ORTHOCH01.htm
US Army Medical Department Office of Medical History - Orthopedic Surgery

http://www.thepeerage.com/ (Genealogical survey of peerage of Britain)

http://qrrarchive.websds.net/ (War Diaries of the East Surrey Regiment)

http://www.anzacsite.gov.au/5environment/nurses/third-agh.html
(3rd Australian General Hospital on Lemnos)

http://www.anzacs.org/pages/AOvassy.html (Lieutenant Vassy on HS Formosa)

http://www.westernfrontassociation.com/ (Multiple use)

http://www.walmerweb.co.uk/history/generals-meadow.html (Story of John Pearcy)

http://www.aim25.ac.uk/cgi-bin/vcdf/detail?coll_id=10219&inst_id=9, (Sir Berkeley Moynihan)

http://livesonline.rcseng.ac.uk/biogs/E000226b.htm (Sir Berkeley Moynihan)

http://www.bmj.com/content/1/2879/333.full.pdf+html B. Moynihan, 'An Address on the Treatment of Gunshot Wounds', British Medical Journal, Vol.1, 4 March 1916, pp.333–339

http://www.kilmerhouse.com, (Carrel-Dakin apparatus)

http://www.rootsweb.ancestry.com/~nzlwo/ West Otago – 150 years of Farming and Families by Amanda Rodger Dickson (New Zealand nurses)

http://libcudl.colorado.edu/wwi/pdf/i73730658.pdf
(An Orthopedic Surgeon's Story of the Great War by H Winnett Orr MD Lincoln, Nebraska December 1921)

http://freespace.virgin.net/labwise.history6/rentrick.htm (Leeds Rent Strike) http://www.gallipoli-association.org/ (Multiple use)

http://www.wwwmp.co.uk/ (West Wales War Memorial Project)

http://rcnarchive.rcn.org.uk/data/VOLUME059-1917/page284-volume59-03rdnovember1917.pdf (mentions Sister M Storey, Asst Matron)

http://www.nzhistory.net.nz/page/anzac-soldiers-riot-cairos-wazzir-brothel-district (Anzac soldiers riot in Cairo)

http://www.camc.wordpress.com, Canadian Expeditionary Force

http://www.vlib.us/medical/CCS/ccs.htm (Locations of CCS in France)

http://en.wikipedia.org/wiki/Indian_Army_during_World_War_I#cite_note-su6-29 (Indian Army in WW1)

http://www.lginursesleague.org.uk/history/ (Nurses at the LGI)

http://www.christies.com/lotfinder/LotDetailsPrintable.aspx?intObjectID=1705161 (Campaign medals of Sir Harold Graham-Hodgson)

http://pmj.bmj.com/ Postgraduate Medical Journal

http://www.nam.ac.uk/ National Army Museum

http://www.britmedals.co.uk/ Britannia Military Antiques

http://www.historyireland.com/20th-century-contemporary-history/the-other-women-of-1916/ (Violet Barrett, drowned after torpedo attack)

http://www.leeds-pals.com/ (Leeds Pals)

STORIES FROM THE
WAR HOSPITAL